THE CATHOLIC WAY JOURNAL

Douay-Rheims Edition
By J. M. Grin

**Remember,
O' Christian Soul,
That this very day,
And every day of thy life,
Thou hast:**

*God to glorify,
Jesus to imitate,
The Angels & Saints to invoke,
A soul to save,
A body to mortify,
Sins to expiate,
Virtue to acquire,
Hell to avoid,
Heaven to gain,
Eternity to prepare for,
Time to profit by,
Neighbours to edify,
The world to despise,
Devils to combat,
Passions to subdue,
Death perhaps to suffer,
And Judgement to undergo.*

AMEN

*Supernatural life is given to man in this life [by God] and what one does
with it is the primary story of one's life. Everything else is incidental,
on the fringe, and of no permanent importance.*
Frank Sheed

DAY

"Let me hear in the morning of Thy steadfast love, for in Thee do I trust.
Make me know the way I should go, for to Thee I lift up my soul."
Psalm 143:8

CONTEMPLATIONS

____

____

____

____

____

____

____

RESOLUTIONS

____

____

____

____

____

____

____

O' my God: Henceforth I resolve to strive earnestly to be patient & gentle,
not allowing the waters of contradiction to extinguish the fire of that
charity which I owe to my neighbour.
St. Francis de Sales, *pray for us.*
AMEN

INVOCATIONS

I. My God, grant that I may love Thee, and let the only
reward of my love be to love Thee more & more.
AMEN

II. My God, make us to be of one mind in the Truth
and of one heart in Charity.
AMEN

NIGHT

Psalm 1:1-2

RECOLLECTIONS

____

____

____

____

EXAMEN
PRIDE - ANGER - LUST - ENVY - GREED - GLUTTONY - SLOTH

____

____

____

____

____

"O' LORD, rebuke me not in Thy indignation, nor chastise me in Thy wrath.
Have mercy on me, O' LORD, for I am weak: heal me, O' LORD
for my bones are troubled. And my soul is troubled exceedingly:
but Thou, O' LORD, how long?"
Psalm 6:1-3

MEDITATIONS

____

____

____

____

PRAYER
Come to us, Holy Spirit, come, One with the Father and the Son.
Vouchsafe to dwell within our souls and quickly make our hearts Thine
own. Let voice & mind, and heart & strength, confess and glorify Thy
name, and let the fire of charity burn bright, so that other hearts inflame.
AMEN

DAY

"Because of the LORD's great love we are not consumed, for His compassions
never fail. They are new every morning; great is Thy faithfulness."
Lamentations 3:22-23

CONTEMPLATIONS

____

____

____

____

____

____

____

RESOLUTIONS

____

____

____

____

____

____

____

____

O' LORD God: give me strength to keep these holy resolutions. If I persevere
in them, I entreat Thee to fill my heart with those consolations
compared to which all others are poor & imperfect.

AMEN

INVOCATION

Come O' Holy Ghost. Fill the hearts of Thy faithful and kindle in them the
fire of Thy love. Send forth Thy Spirit and they shall be created anew.
And Thou shalt renew the face of the earth.

O' God, whom by the light of the Holy Ghost, did instruct the hearts of the
faithful, grant that by the same Holy Spirit we may be truly wise and ever
enjoy His consolations, Through Christ Our Lord.

AMEN

NIGHT

*"Let Thy ears be attentive, and Thy eyes open, to hear the prayer of Thy servant,
which I pray before Thee now, night & day… and I confess the sins of
the children of Israel, by which they have sinned against Thee:
I and my father's house have sinned. "*
Nehemiah 1:6

RECOLLECTIONS

EXAMEN
PRIDE - ANGER - LUST - ENVY - GREED - GLUTTONY - SLOTH

"Turn to me, O' LORD, and deliver my soul: O' save me for Thy mercy's
sake. For in death there is no one that is mindful of Thee:
and who shall confess to Thee in Hell?"
Psalm 6:4-5

MEDITATIONS

PRAYER
O' God, Who hast doomed all men to die, but hast concealed
from all the hour of their death, grant that I may pass
my days in the practice of holiness & justice:
That I may deserve to depart this world in the peace of a good conscience,
and in the embraces of Thy love. Through Christ Our Lord.
AMEN

DAY

*"O' LORD, in the morning you hear my voice; in the morning
I prepare a sacrifice for Thee and watch."*
Psalm 5:3

CONTEMPLATIONS

____

____

____

____

____

____

RESOLUTIONS

____

____

____

____

____

____

Love and do what you will. Therefore, once for all, this short command is
given to us: *'Love and do what you will'*.
If you keep silent, keep silent by love: if you speak, speak by love; if you
correct, correct by love; if you pardon, pardon by love; let love be rooted in
Thee, my God, and from this root nothing but good can grow.
St. Augustine of Hippo, *pray for us.*
AMEN

INVOCATIONS

I. My God, I give Thee thanks for what Thou givest,
and for what Thou takest away; Thy will be done.
AMEN

II. With all my heart & voice, I acknowledge, praise and bless Thee,
God the Father unbegotten, Thee, the only-begotten Son, Thee, the Holy
Ghost the Paraclete, O holy & undivided Trinity.
AMEN

NIGHT

"Behold I command thee, take courage, and be strong.
Fear not and be not dismayed: because the LORD thy GOD is with thee
in all things whatsoever thou shalt undergo."
Joshua 1:9

RECOLLECTIONS

____

____

____

____

EXAMEN
PRIDE - ANGER - LUST - ENVY - GREED - GLUTTONY - SLOTH

____

____

____

____

____

"Blessed are they whose iniquities are forgiven, and whose sins are
covered. Blessed is the man to whom the LORD hath not imputed sin,
and in whose spirit there is no guile."
Psalm 31:1-2

MEDITATIONS

____

____

____

____

____

PRAYER
Great God, Lord of Heaven & Earth! I prostrate myself before Thee.
With all the Angels & Saints I adore Thee. I acknowledge Thee to be my
Creator and Sovereign Lord, my first beginning and last end. I render to
Thee the homage of my being and life, I submit myself to Thy holy Will,
and I devote myself to Thy divine service, now and for ever.
AMEN

DAY

*"The sun rises, and the sun goes down, and hastens to the place where it rises.
The wind blows to the south and goes around to the north; around and around
goes the wind, and on its circuits the wind returns. All streams run to the sea,
but the sea is not full; to the place where the streams flow, there they flow again."*
Ecclesiastes 1:5-7

CONTEMPLATIONS

____

____

____

____

____

____

RESOLUTIONS

____

____

____

____

____

____

____

My Saviour! I cheerfully accept all of the painful dispositions,
in which it is Thy will to place me.
My wish is in all things to conform myself to Thy holy will…
St. Margaret Mary Alacoque, *pray for us.*
AMEN

INVOCATION

May the Lord Jesus Christ be with me, that he may defend me; may He be
within me, that he may conserve me; may He be before me, that He may
lead me; may He be behind me, so that He guard me; may He be above
me, that He may bless me, Whom with God the Father and Holy Ghost,
lives & reigns forever & ever.
AMEN

NIGHT

*"And will not GOD revenge His elect who cry to Him day & night,
and will He delay long over them?"*
Luke 18:7

RECOLLECTIONS

____

____

____

____

EXAMEN
PRIDE - ANGER - LUST - ENVY - GREED - GLUTTONY - SLOTH

____

____

____

____

"I have acknowledged my sin to Thee, and my injustice I have not
concealed. I said: *I will confess against myself, my injustices to the LORD…*
and Thou hast forgiven the wickedness of my sin."
Psalm 31:5-6

MEDITATIONS

____

____

____

____

PRAYER
Eternal God, come down into my soul, that all my enemies may
be driven out; all my crimes melted away; all my sins forgiven.

Enlighten my understanding with the light of true faith; inflame my will
with Thy sweet love; clear up my mind with Thy glad presence;
and give virtue to all my powers. Watch over me especially at my death,
that I may come to enjoy Thy beatific vision in eternal bliss.
AMEN

DAY

"I wait for the LORD, my soul waits, and in His word I hope;
my soul waits for the LORD more than watchmen for the morning,
more than watchmen for the morning."
Psalm 130:6

CONTEMPLATIONS

____

____

____

____

____

____

RESOLUTIONS

____

____

____

____

____

____

Father, I dedicate this new day to you; as I go about my work. I ask you to
bless those with whom I come into contact. Lord, I pray for all men &
women who work to earn their living; give them satisfaction in what they
do. Spirit of God, comfort the unemployed and their families;
they too are your children and my brothers & sisters.
I ask you to help them find work soon.
St. Ignatius of Loyola, *pray for us.*
AMEN

INVOCATIONS

I. May the most just, the most high and most admirable will of God be in
all things done, praised and exalted evermore.
AMEN

II. Teach me, O' Lord, to do Thy will, for Thou alone art my God.
AMEN

NIGHT

*"Every best gift, and every perfect gift, is from above, coming down from the
Father of lights, with whom there is no change, nor shadow of alteration.
For of His own will hath He begotten us by the Word of Truth,
that we might be some beginning of His creatures."*
James 1:17-18

RECOLLECTIONS

EXAMEN
PRIDE - ANGER - LUST - ENVY - GREED - GLUTTONY - SLOTH

"Rebuke me not, O' LORD, in Thy indignation; nor chastise me in Thy
wrath. For Thy arrows are fastened in me: and Thy hand hath been strong
upon me. There is no health in my flesh, because of Thy wrath:
there is no peace for my bones, because of my sins."
Psalm 38:1-3

MEDITATIONS

PRAYER
Be mindful, O' Lord, of Thy creature,
whom Thou hast redeemed by Thy Precious Blood.
Eternal Father, I offer Thee the Precious Blood of my Lord Jesus Christ
in atonement for my sins and the sins of the whole world.
Have mercy on us all.
AMEN

DAY

"Satisfy us in the morning with Thy steadfast love, that we may rejoice and be glad all our days. Make us glad for as many days as Thou hast afflicted us, and for as many years as we have seen evil."
Psalm 90:14-15

CONTEMPLATIONS

____

____

____

____

____

RESOLUTIONS

____

____

____

____

____

Jesus, Name full of glory, grace, love and strength!
Thou art the refuge of those who mourn, the delight of those who repent,
our banner of warfare in this life, the medicine of souls, the comfort of
those who mourn, the delight of those who believe, the light of those who
preach the true faith, the wages of those who toil, the healing of the sick.
To Thee our devotion aspires; by Thee our prayers are received;
we delight in contemplating Thee. O' Name of Jesus,
Thou art the glory of all the saints for eternity.
St. Bernadine, *pray for us.*
AMEN

INVOCATIONS

I. Keep me, O' Lord, as the apple of Thine eye;
beneath the shadow of Thy wings protect me.
AMEN

II. Into Thy Hands, O' Lord, I commend my spirit.
AMEN

III. Vouchsafe, O' Lord, this day to keep me without sin.
AMEN

NIGHT

*"Give glory to the LORD, for He is good: for His mercy endureth for ever.
Let them say so that have been redeemed by the LORD, whom He hath redeemed
from the hand of the enemy… From the rising and the setting of the sun,
from the north and from the sea."*
Psalm 107:1-3

RECOLLECTIONS

____

____

____

____

EXAMEN
PRIDE - ANGER - LUST - ENVY - GREED - GLUTTONY - SLOTH

____

____

____

____

"For my iniquities are gone over my head:
and as a heavy burden are become heavy upon me.
My sores are putrified and corrupted, because of my foolishness.
I am become miserable, and am bowed down even to the end."
Psalm 38:4-6

MEDITATIONS

____

____

____

____

PRAYERS

I. O' Lord, reward us not according to our sins of which we are guilty,
neither according to our iniquities.
AMEN

II. Lord, I fear Thy justice, I implore Thy mercy; deliver me not to
everlasting pains, but grant that I may possess
Thee in the midst of everlasting joys.
AMEN

DAY

"Sing praises to the LORD, O' you His saints, and give thanks to His holy name.
For His anger is but for a moment, and His favor is for a lifetime.
Weeping may tarry for the night, but joy comes with the morning."
Psalm 30:5

CONTEMPLATIONS

____

____

____

____

____

____

RESOLUTIONS

____

____

____

____

____

____

____

Lord, I am in this world to show Thy mercy to others. Other people will glorify Thee by making visible the power of Thy grace, by their fidelity & constancy to Thee. For my part, I will glorify Thee by making known how good Thou art to sinners, that Thy mercy is boundless and that no sinner, no matter how great, should have reason to despair of Thy pardon…
St. Claude de la Colombiere, *pray for us.*
AMEN

INVOCATION

My God, I believe in Thee, I hope in Thee, I love Thee above all things with all my soul, with all my heart and with all my strength; I love Thee because Thou art infinitely good and worthy of all love.

Because I love Thee, I repent with all my heart of having offended Thee; have mercy on me, a sinner.
AMEN

NIGHT

"Holy, Holy, Holy is the LORD GOD Almighty,
who was, and who is, and who is to come."
Apocalypse 4:8

RECOLLECTIONS

EXAMEN
PRIDE - ANGER - LUST - ENVY - GREED - GLUTTONY - SLOTH

"Thou shalt sprinkle me with hyssop, and I shall be cleansed:
Thou shalt wash me, and I shall be made whiter than snow.
To my hearing Thou shalt give me joy and gladness:
and the bones that have been humbled shall rejoice."
Psalm 51:7-8

MEDITATIONS

PRAYER

Holy God, Holy Mighty One, Holy Immortal One,
have mercy on us and on the whole world.
To Thee be praise, to Thee be glory, to Thee be thanksgiving
through endless ages, O' Holy Trinity.
AMEN

DAY

"The LORD is my shepherd; I shall not want. He makes me to lie down in green pastures. He leads me beside still waters. He restores my soul. He leads me in paths of righteousness for His name's sake."
Psalm 23:1-3

CONTEMPLATIONS

____

____

____

____

____

____

RESOLUTIONS

____

____

____

____

____

____

Grant me, O' Lord my God, a mind to know Thee, a heart to seek Thee, wisdom to find Thee, conduct pleasing to Thee, faithful perseverance in waiting for Thee, and a hope of finally embracing Thee.
St. Thomas Aquinas, *pray for us.*
AMEN

INVOCATIONS

I. Almighty and everlasting God, give unto us an increase of Faith, Hope and Charity; and, that we may deserve to obtain that which Thou dost promise, make us to love that which Thou dost command. Through Christ our Lord.
AMEN

II. I believe in Thee, I hope in Thee, I love Thee, I adore Thee, O' Blessed Trinity, one God; have mercy on me now and at the hour of my death, save me.
AMEN

NIGHT

"Come to Me, all you that labour, and are burdened, and I will refresh you. Take up My yoke upon you, and learn of Me, because I am meek, and humble of heart: and you shall find rest for your souls. For My yoke is sweet and my burden light."
Matthew 11:28

RECOLLECTIONS

EXAMEN
PRIDE - ANGER - LUST - ENVY - GREED - GLUTTONY - SLOTH

"Have mercy on me, O' GOD, according to Thy great mercy.
And according to the multitude of Thy tender mercies blot out my iniquity.
Wash me yet more from my iniquity, and cleanse me from my sin"
Psalm 51:1-2

MEDITATIONS

PRAYER

My Lord Jesus Christ, Son of the living God, I humbly ask of Thee to scatter the darkness of my mind, and to give me a lively faith, a firm hope and a burning love. Grant, O' my God, that I may know Thee well and may do all things in Thy light and in conformity to Thy holy will.
AMEN

DAY

"But I will sing of Thy strength; I will sing aloud of Thy steadfast love in the morning. For Thou hast been to me a fortress and a refuge in the day of my distress. O' my Strength, I will sing Thy praise, for Thee, O' GOD, are my fortress, the God who shows me steadfast love."
Psalm 59:16

CONTEMPLATIONS

RESOLUTIONS

Take, O' Lord, and receive all my liberty, my memory, my understanding, and my whole will. Thou hast given me all that I am and all that I possess: I surrender it all to Thee that Thou mayest dispose of it according to Thy will. Give me only Thy love & Thy grace; with these I will be rich enough, and will have no more to desire.
St. Ignatius of Antioch, *pray for us.*
AMEN

INVOCATIONS

I. Jesus Christ, Son of the living God, light of the world,
I adore Thee; for Thee do I live, for Thee I die.
AMEN

II. Jesus, I live for Thee; Jesus, I die for Thee;
Jesus I am Thine both in life and in death.
AMEN

NIGHT

"But Thou, O' LORD art my protector, my glory, and the lifter up of my head.
I have cried to the LORD with my voice: and He hath heard me from His holy hill."
Psalm 3:3-4

RECOLLECTIONS

____

____

____

____

EXAMEN
PRIDE - ANGER - LUST - ENVY - GREED - GLUTTONY - SLOTH

____

____

____

____

____

"For I am ready for scourges: and my sorrow is continually before me.
For I will declare my inequity: and I will think for my sin…
Forsake me not, O' LORD, my GOD: do not Thou depart from me.
Attend unto my help, O' LORD, the GOD of my Salvation."
Psalm 38:17-18, 21-22

MEDITATIONS

____

____

____

____

PRAYERS

I. O' my Jesus, Thou who art Love Itself, enkindle in my heart that divine fire which consumes the Saints and transforms souls into Thy likeness.
AMEN

II. Jesus, for love of Thee, with Thee and for Thee.
AMEN

DAY

"Who is this that both wind and sea obey Him?"
Mark 4:41

CONTEMPLATIONS

RESOLUTIONS

Steer the ship of my life, good Lord, to Thy quiet harbour, where I can be
safe from the storms of sin & conflict. Show me the course I should take.
Renew in me the gift of discernment, so that I can always see the right
direction in which I should go. And give me the strength and the courage
to choose the right course, even when the sea is rough and the waves are
high, knowing that through enduring both hardship & danger, in Thy
name, we shall find comfort & peace.
St. Basil of Caesarea, *pray for us.*
AMEN

INVOCATIONS
From all evil, deliver us, O' Lord.
From all sin, deliver us, O' Lord.
From Thy wrath, deliver us, O' Lord.
From sudden & unprovided death, deliver us, O' Lord.
From the snares of the devil, deliver us, O' Lord.
From anger, hatred, and all ill will, deliver us, O' Lord.
From impure spirits, deliver us, O' Lord.
From lightning & tempest, deliver us, O' Lord.
From plague, famine, and wars, deliver us, O' Lord.
From everlasting fire, deliver us, O' Lord.
AMEN

NIGHT

*"If thou sleep, thou shalt not fear: thou shalt rest, and thy sleep shall be sweet.
Be not afraid of sudden fear, nor of the power of the wicked falling upon thee.
For the LORD will be at thy side, and will keep thy foot that thou be not taken."*
Proverbs 3:24-26

RECOLLECTIONS

____

____

____

____

EXAMEN
PRIDE - ANGER - LUST - ENVY - GREED - GLUTTONY - SLOTH

____

____

____

____

____

"For I know my iniquity, and my sin is always before me. To Thee only
have I sinned, and have done evil before Thee: that Thou mayst be justified
in Thy words and mayst overcome when Thou art contradicted."
Psalm 51:3-4

MEDITATIONS

____

____

____

____

PRAYERS

I. O' my Jesus, Son of the living God, light of the world, I adore Thee;
for Thee I live, for Thee I die.
AMEN

II. Visit, we beseech Thee, O' Lord, this dwelling, and drive far from it all
snares of the enemy; let Thy holy Angels dwell herein, to preserve us in
peace; and let Thy blessing be always upon us. Through Christ our Lord.
AMEN

DAY

*"All things have their season, and in their times all things pass under heaven.
A time to be born and a time to die. A time to plant, and a time to pluck up that
which is planted. A time to kill, and a time to heal. A time to destroy, and a time to
build. A time to weep, and a time to laugh. A time to mourn, and a time to dance.
A time to scatter stones, and a time to gather. A time to embrace, and a time to be
far from embraces. A time to get, and a time to lose. A time to keep, and a time to
cast away. A time to rend, and a time to sew. A time to keep silence, and a time to
speak. A time of love, and a time of hatred. A time of war, and a time of peace."*
Ecclesiastes 3:1-8

CONTEMPLATIONS

____

____

____

____

____

RESOLUTIONS

____

____

____

____

Let me bless Almighty God, Whose power extends over sea & land, whose
angels watch over all. Let me study the sacred books to calm my soul: I
pray for peace, kneeling at Heaven's gates. Let me do my daily work —
Let me give to the poor. Let me say my daily prayers, always thanking
God. Delightful it is to live, serving the King of kings.
St. Columba, *pray for us.*
AMEN

INVOCATION

O' dearly beloved Word of God, teach me to be generous, to serve Thee as
Thou dost deserve, to give without counting the cost, to fight without
fretting at my wounds, to labour without seeking repose, to be prodigal of
myself without looking for any other reward save
that of knowing that I do Thy Holy Will.
AMEN

NIGHT

"To Thee have I lifted up my eyes, who dwellest in Heaven. Behold as the eyes
of the servants are on the hands of their masters… so are our eyes
unto the LORD our God, until He have mercy on us."
Psalm 123:1-2

RECOLLECTIONS

EXAMEN
PRIDE - ANGER - LUST - ENVY - GREED - GLUTTONY - SLOTH

"For behold I was conceived in iniquities; and in sins did my mother
conceive me. For behold Thou hast loved Truth: the uncertain
and hidden things of Thy wisdom Thou hast made manifest to me."
Psalm 51:5-6

MEDITATIONS

PRAYER

Lamb of God, Who takes away the sins of the world, spare us, O' Lord.
Lamb of God, Who takes away the sins of the world, hear us, O' Lord.
Lamb of God, Who takes away the sins of the world, have mercy on us.
AMEN

DAY

"Keep thy foot, when thou goest into the house of GOD, and draw nigh to hear. For much better is obedience, than the sacrifices of fools, who know not what evil they do. Speak nothing rashly, and let not thy heart be hasty to utter a word before GOD. For GOD is in Heaven, and thou upon Earth: therefore let thy words be few."
Ecclesiastes 5:1-2

CONTEMPLATIONS

____

____

____

____

____

RESOLUTIONS

____

____

____

____

____

Lord, make me an instrument of Thy peace. Where there is hatred, let me sow love; where there is injury, pardon; where there is doubt, faith; where there is despair, hope; where there is darkness, light; where there is sadness, joy.
O' Divine Master, grant that I may not so much seek to be consoled, as to console; to be understood, as to understand; to be loved, as to love with all my soul. For it is in giving that we receive; it is in pardoning that we are pardoned; and it is in dying that we are born to eternal life.
St. Francis of Assisi, *pray for us.*
AMEN

INVOCATION

Change my heart, O Jesus, Thou who didst empty Thyself for love of me! Make known to my spirit how excellent were Thy sacred humiliations. Let me begin this day, illumined by Thy Divine light, to do away with any portion of the natural man, that still lives undiminished in me. This is the chief source of my misery, the barrier that I constantly oppose to Thy love.
AMEN

NIGHT

*"Let not mercy and truth leave thee, but put them about thy neck,
and write them in the tables of thy heart: And thou shalt have grace
and good understanding before GOD and men."*
Proverbs 3:3-4

RECOLLECTIONS

EXAMEN
PRIDE - ANGER - LUST - ENVY - GREED - GLUTTONY - SLOTH

"For my loins are filled with illusions; and there is no health in my flesh.
I am afflicted and humbled exceedingly: I roared with the groaning of my
heart. LORD, all my desire is before Thee, and my
groaning is not hidden from Thee."
Psalm 38:7-9

MEDITATIONS

PRAYERS

I. O' Good Jesus, hide me in Thy Sacred Heart, permit me not
to be separated from Thee, defend me from the evil one.
AMEN

II. We adore Thee, most holy Lord Jesus Christ, here in this household
and in all Thy churches that are in the whole world.
We bless Thee; for by Thy holy cross Thou hast redeemed the world.
AMEN

DAY

"What gain have the workers for their toils? I have seen the labour that GOD has given to the sons of men to be busied with. He hath made all things good in their time, and hath delivered the world to their consideration, so that man cannot find out the work which GOD hath made from the beginning to the end."
Ecclesiastes 3:9-11

CONTEMPLATIONS

____

____

____

____

____

RESOLUTIONS

____

____

____

____

O' Sacred Heart of Jesus, fount of eternal life, Thy Heart is a glowing furnace of Love. Thou art my refuge & sanctuary. O' my adorable & loving Saviour, consume my heart with the burning fire with which Thine own is inflamed. Pour down on my soul those graces which flow from Thy Love. Let my heart be united with Thine. Let my will be conformed to Thine in all things. May Thy will be the rule of all of my desires & actions.
St. Gertrude the Great, *pray for us.*
AMEN

INVOCATIONS

I. O' Lord, reward us not according to our sins,
of which we are guilty, neither according to our iniquities.
AMEN

II. Abide with me, O' Lord, be Thou my true joy.
AMEN

III. May the most just, the most high and the most lovable will of God be in all things done, praised and evermore exalted.
AMEN

NIGHT

*"But the things that are in Heaven, who shall search out? And who shall know
Thy thought, except Thou give wisdom, and send Thy Holy Spirit from above:
And so the ways of them that are upon earth may be corrected,
and men may learn the things that please Thee?"*
Wisdom 9:16-19

RECOLLECTIONS

EXAMEN
PRIDE - ANGER - LUST - ENVY - GREED - GLUTTONY - SLOTH

---

*"Hear me speedily, O' LORD: my spirit hath fainted away. Turn not away
Thy face from me, lest I be like unto them that go down into the pit.
Cause me to hear Thy mercy in the morning; for in Thee have I hoped.
Make the way known to me, wherein I should walk:
for I have lifted up my soul to Thee."*
Psalm 133:7-8

MEDITATIONS

PRAYER
Deliver me, Lord Jesus Christ, from all of my
iniquities and from every evil. Make me ever hold fast to
Thy commandments and never allow me to be separated from Thee.
AMEN

DAY

"For wrath is in his indignation; and life in his good will.
In the evening weeping shall have place, and in the morning gladness.
And in my abundance I said: I shall never be moved."
Psalm 30:5-6

CONTEMPLATIONS

____

____

____

____

____

RESOLUTIONS

____

____

____

____

____

Christ with me, Christ before me, Christ behind me, Christ in me, Christ beneath me, Christ above me, Christ on my right, Christ on my left, Christ where I lie, Christ where I sit, Christ where I arise, Christ in the heart of everyone who thinks of me, Christ in the mouth of everyone who speaks to me, Christ in every eye that sees me, Christ in every ear that hears me.
Salvation is of the Lord. Salvation is of the Christ.
May Thy salvation, Lord, be ever with us.
St. Patrick, *pray for us.*
AMEN

INVOCATION

O' Lord Omnipotent, who permits evil that Thou mayest draw good therefrom, give ear to our humble petitions, whereby we beg of Thee the grace of being faithful unto death, evermore conforming ourselves to Thy most Holy Will.
AMEN

NIGHT

"I have lifted up my eyes to the mountains, from whence help shall come to me. My help is from the LORD, who made Heaven & Earth... Behold He shall neither slumber nor sleep, that keepeth Israel. The LORD is thy keeper, the LORD is thy protection upon thy right hand. The sun shall not burn thee by day: nor the moon by night. The LORD keepeth thee from all evil: may the LORD keep thy soul."
Psalm 121:1-7

RECOLLECTIONS

____

____

____

____

EXAMEN
PRIDE - ANGER - LUST - ENVY - GREED - GLUTTONY - SLOTH

____

____

____

____

____

"Turn away Thy face from my sins, and blot out all of my iniquities. Create a clean heart in me, O' GOD and renew a right spirit within my bowels. Cast me not away from Thy face; and take not Thy Holy Spirit from me."
Psalm 51:9-11

MEDITATIONS

____

____

____

____

____

PRAYER
Jesus Christ my God, I adore Thee and thank Thee for all the graces Thou hast given me this day. I offer Thee my sleep and all the moments of this night, and I beseech Thee to keep me without sin.
AMEN

DAY

*"You, LORD, are a shield around me, my glory, and the One who lifts my head.
I lay down and slept; I awoke, for the LORD sustains me. I will not be afraid of
ten thousands of people who have set themselves against me all around."*
Psalm 3:3, 5-6

CONTEMPLATIONS

____

____

____

____

____

____

____

RESOLUTIONS

____

____

____

____

____

____

____

Govern everything by Thy wisdom, O' LORD, so that my soul may always
be serving Thee in the way of Thy will and not as I choose. Let me die to
myself so that I may serve Thee; let me live to Thee who art life itself.
St. Theresa of Avila, *pray for us.*
AMEN

INVOCATIONS

I. Blessed be the most Holy Name of Jesus without end!
AMEN

II. O Holy Spirit, Spirit of truth, come into our hearts;
shed the brightness of Thy light upon the nations,
that they may please Thee in unity of faith.
AMEN

NIGHT

"Blessed are all they that Fear the LORD: *that walk in his ways. For thou shalt eat the labours of thy hands: blessed art thou, and it shall be well with thee."*
Psalm 128:1-2

RECOLLECTIONS

____

____

____

____

EXAMEN
PRIDE - ANGER - LUST - ENVY - GREED - GLUTTONY - SLOTH

____

____

____

____

"Restore unto me the joy of Thy Salvation, and strengthen me with a
perfect spirit. I will teach the unjust Thy ways: and the wicked
shall be converted to Thee. Deliver me from blood, O' GOD,
Thou GOD of my Salvation: and my tongue shall extol Thy justice. O' LORD,
Thou wilt open my lips: and my mouth shall declare Thy praise"
Psalm 51:12-15

MEDITATIONS

____

____

____

____

PRAYER

O' my God, at the end of this day I thank Thee most heartily for all the
graces I have received from Thee. I am sorry that I have not made better
use of them. I am sorry for all the sins I have committed against Thee.
Forgive me, O' my God, and graciously protect me this night.
AMEN

DAY

"But I will sing of your strength; I will sing aloud of your steadfast love in the morning. For you have been to me a fortress and a refuge in the day of my distress. O' my Strength, I will sing praises to you, for you, O' GOD, are my fortress, the GOD who shows me steadfast love."
Psalm 59:16

CONTEMPLATIONS

RESOLUTIONS

May God the Father bless us, may Christ take care of us,
May the Holy Ghost enlighten us all the days of our life.
The Lord be our defender and keeper of body and soul,
Both now & forever, to the ages of ages.
St. Ethelwold, *pray for us.*
AMEN

INVOCATION

Lord God Almighty,
who hast safely brought us to the beginning of this day,
defend us in the same by Thy mighty power,
that this day we may fall into no sin,
but that all our words may so proceed,
and all our thoughts and actions may be so directed
as to do always that which is just in Thy sight.

AMEN

NIGHT

"My [child], if thou wilt receive my words, and wilt hide my commandments with thee, That thy ear may hearken to wisdom: Incline thy heart to know prudence: For if thou shalt call for wisdom, and incline thy heart to prudence: If thou shalt seek her as money, and shalt dig for her as for a treasure: Then shalt thou understand the fear of the LORD, and shalt find the knowledge of GOD."
Proverbs 2:1-5

RECOLLECTIONS

EXAMEN
PRIDE - ANGER - LUST - ENVY - GREED - GLUTTONY - SLOTH

"For if Thou hadst desired sacrifice, I would indeed have given it: with burnt offerings Thou wilt not be delighted. A sacrifice to GOD is an afflicted spirit: a contrite and humbled heart, O' GOD, Thou wilt not despise."
Psalm 51:16-17

MEDITATIONS

PRAYER

Most Sacred Heart of Jesus! I select Thee as my resting place, that Thou mayst be my strength in combat, my support in weakness, my light and guide in darkness, the expiation of my faults, and the sanctification of my intentions and actions, which I unite with Thine.
AMEN

DAY

"And in the way of Thy judgments, O' LORD, we have patiently waited for Thee:
Thy name, and Thy remembrance are the desire of the soul.
My soul hath desired Thee in the night: yea, and with my spirit within me in the
morning early I will watch to Thee. When Thou shalt do Thy judgments on the
earth, the inhabitants of the world shall learn justice."
Isaiah 26:8-9

CONTEMPLATIONS

____

____

____

____

RESOLUTIONS

____

____

____

____

____

O' Lord my God. Teach me this day where and how to find Thee.
Thou hast made and re-made me, and Thou hast bestowed on me all the
good things I possess, and still I do not know Thee as a I should.
I have not yet done that for which I was made.
Teach me to seek Thee, for I cannot seek Thee unless Thou teachest me,
or find Thee unless Thou showest Thyself to me. Let me seek Thee in my
desire; let me desire Thee in my seeking. Let me find Thee by loving Thee;
let me love Thee when I find Thee.
St. Anselm, *pray for us.*
AMEN

INVOCATION

Visit, we beseech Thee, O' Lord, this dwelling, and drive far from it all
snares of the enemy. Let Thy holy Angels dwell herein,
to preserve us in peace; and let Thy blessing be always upon us.
Through Christ our Lord.
AMEN

NIGHT

"Because the Lord giveth wisdom: and out of his mouth cometh prudence and knowledge. He will keep the salvation of the righteous, and protect them that walk in simplicity. Keeping the paths of justice, and guarding the ways of saints. Then shalt thou understand justice, and judgment, and equity, and every good path."
Proverbs 2:6-9

RECOLLECTIONS

____

____

____

____

EXAMEN
PRIDE - ANGER - LUST - ENVY - GREED - GLUTTONY - SLOTH

____

____

____

____

"Hear, O' LORD, my prayer: and let my cry come to Thee. Turn not away Thy face from me: in the day when I am in trouble, incline Thy ear to me. In what day soever I shall call upon Thee, hear me speedily."
Psalm 102:1-2

MEDITATIONS

____

____

____

____

PRAYER

Vouchsafe, O Lord, this night, to keep us without sin.
Have mercy upon us, O Lord.
Have mercy upon us.
Let Thy mercy be upon us, O Lord,
As we have hoped in Thee.
AMEN

DAY

"Knowest thou not, or hast thou not heard? The Lord is the everlasting GOD,
who hath created the ends of the earth: he shall not faint, nor labour,
neither is there any searching out of his wisdom. It is he that giveth strength
to the weary, and increaseth force and might to them that are not."
Isaiah 40:28-29

CONTEMPLATIONS

____

____

____

____

____

____

RESOLUTIONS

____

____

____

____

____

____

Let Thy divinity shine on my intellect by giving it divine knowledge,
and on my will by imparting to it the divine love, and on my memory with
the divine possession of glory. Let us so act that by means of this loving
activity we may attain to the vision of… Thy beauty in eternal life…
St. John of the Cross, *pray for us.*
AMEN

INVOCATIONS

I. O Holy Spirit, Spirit of Truth, come into our hearts; shed the brightness
of Thy light upon the nations, that they may please Thee in unity of Faith.
AMEN

II. O Holy Spirit, sweet Guest of my soul,
abide in me and grant that I may ever abide in Thee.
AMEN

III. God the Holy Ghost, have mercy on us.
AMEN

NIGHT

"If wisdom shall enter into thy heart, and knowledge please thy soul:
Counsel shall keep thee, and prudence shall preserve thee,
That thou mayst be delivered from the evil way."
Proverbs 2:10-12

RECOLLECTIONS

EXAMEN
PRIDE - ANGER - LUST - ENVY - GREED - GLUTTONY - SLOTH

"For my days are vanished like smoke: and my bones are grown dry
like fuel for the fire. I am smitten as grass, and my heart is withered:
because I forgot to eat my bread. Through the voice of my groaning,
my bone hath cleaved to my flesh."
Psalm 102:3-5

MEDITATIONS

PRAYER

O my Lord Jesus Christ, Judge of the living and the dead,
before Whom I must appear one day to give an exact account of my whole
life; enlighten me, I beseech Thee, and give me a humble and contrite
heart, that I may see wherein I have offended Thine infinite Majesty,
and judge myself now with such a just severity, that then Thou mayest
judge me with mercy and clemency.
AMEN

DAY

"For I know the plans that I have for you, saith the LORD. *Plans of peace,
and not of affliction, to give you an end and patience. And you shall call upon me,
and you shall go: and you shall pray to me, and I will hear you. You shall seek me,
and shall find me: when you shall seek me with all your heart."*
Jeremiah 29:11-13

CONTEMPLATIONS

____

____

____

____

____

____

RESOLUTIONS

____

____

____

____

____

____

O Lord and Master of my life, a spirit of idleness, curiosity, ambition,
and idle talking; give me not. But a spirit of chastity, humility, patience,
and love, bestow upon me, Thy servant.
Yea, O Lord, my King: grant me to see mine own failings,
and not to condemn others; for blessed art Thou unto the ages of ages.
St. Ephrem, *pray for us.*
AMEN

INVOCATION

O Jesus, Son of the living God,
have mercy on us!
Jesus, Son of the Virgin Mary,
have mercy on us!
O Jesus, King and center of all hearts,
grant that peace may be in Thy Kingdom.
AMEN

NIGHT

"I cried to the Lord with my voice; to GOD with my voice, and he gave ear to me. In the day of my trouble I sought GOD, with my hands lifted up to him in the night, and I was not deceived. My soul refused to be comforted: I remembered GOD, and was delighted, and was exercised, and my spirit swooned away."
Psalm 76:1-3

RECOLLECTIONS

EXAMEN
PRIDE - ANGER - LUST - ENVY - GREED - GLUTTONY - SLOTH

"Out of the depths I have cried to Thee, O' LORD: LORD, hear my voice.
Let Thy ears be attentive to the voice of my supplication.
If Thou, O' LORD, wilt mark iniquities: LORD, who shall stand it."
Psalm 130:1-3

MEDITATIONS

PRAYER

Heavenly Father, I thank Thee that Thy Word enlightens my eyes, purifies my soul and preserves me for eternal life. As I reach the end of this day, I thank Thee for the many blessings Thou hast bestowed on me. I ask for forgiveness for the sins I have committed today. I pray that, as I sleep, Thou wouldst restore my strength and empower me for a new day tomorrow. Lord, bless me and keep me, make Thy face shine upon me. Turn Thy face towards me and give me peace.

AMEN

DAY

"The light is sweet, and it is delightful for the eyes to see the sun.
If a man live many years, and have rejoiced in them all, he must remember
the darksome time, and the many days: which when they shall come,
the things past shall be accused of vanity."
Ecclesiastes 11:7-8

CONTEMPLATIONS

RESOLUTIONS

Almighty God, open Thou my heart, and enlighten me with the grace of
the Holy Spirit, to see those things which are well-pleasing to Thy will.
Direct my thoughts and understanding to those things which it is proper to
meditate upon and to take in hand; in such fashion as by fitting character
and deeds, I might be found worthy of the eternal joy of heavenly life.
Direct my acts to thy commandments, that I might by labour so
unbrokenly study to bring them to fulfilment,
as to attain to an everlasting reward.
St. Bede the Venerable, *pray for us.*

INVOCATIONS

I. May the grace of the Holy Spirit enlighten our senses and our hearts.
AMEN

II. May our hearts be cleansed, O Lord, by the inpouring of the Holy Spirit,
and may He render them fruitful by watering them
with His heavenly dew.
AMEN

NIGHT

"The LORD is in his holy temple, the Lord's throne is in heaven.
His eyes look on the poor man: his eyelids examine the sons of men.
The LORD trieth the just and the wicked: but he that loveth iniquity hateth his own
soul. He shall rain snares upon sinners: fire and brimstone and storms of winds
shall be the portion of their cup. For the LORD is just, and hath loved justice:
his countenance hath beheld righteousness."
Psalm 10:4-7

RECOLLECTIONS

EXAMEN
PRIDE - ANGER - LUST - ENVY - GREED - GLUTTONY - SLOTH

"For with Thee there is merciful forgiveness: and by reason of Thy Law,
I have waited for Thee, O' LORD. My soul hath relied on His Word:
my soul hath hoped in the LORD... Because with the LORD there is mercy:
and with Him plentiful redemption."
Psalm 130:4-5, 7

MEDITATIONS

PRAYER

Faithful Father, I thank Thee that Thy work is perfect, Thy ways are just, and Thou
art a God of faithfulness. As I lay down to sleep, I entrust myself into Thy care.
I ask that Thou bringest peace to my mind, rest to my body and restoration to my
spirit. Thou art able to do far more abundantly than all that I ask or imagine,
according to Thy power at work within me. To Thee be glory throughout
all generations, forever and ever.

AMEN

DAY

"Why have the Nations raged, and the people devised vain things? The kings of the earth stood up, and the princes met together, against the LORD and against his Christ. Let us break their bonds asunder: and let us cast away their yoke from us."
Psalm 2:1-3

CONTEMPLATIONS

____

____

____

____

____

RESOLUTIONS

____

____

____

____

____

Let us therefore pray to our Lord Jesus Christ that he give us the grace to seek his Kingdom and to build within ourselves a moral Jerusalem.
By doing this, we will be able to merit our place in the heavenly Jerusalem to sing Alleluia in its streets with all the saints and angels.
But the One whose Kingdom is eternal for all ages must help us to do so.
St. Anthony of Padua, *pray for us.*
AMEN

INVOCATIONS

I. Christ conquers! Christ Reigns! Christ Commands!
AMEN

II. Jesus, King and center of all hearts,
by the coming of Thy Kingdom, grant us peace.
AMEN

NIGHT

"In Thee, O' LORD, I have hoped, let me never be put to confusion: Deliver me in Thy justice, and rescue me. Incline Thy ear unto me, and save me. Be Thou unto me a GOD, a protector, and a place of strength: that Thou mayst make me safe. For Thou art my firmament and my refuge. Deliver me, O my GOD, out of the hand of the wicked, and out of the hand of the transgressor of the law and of the unjust. For thou art my patience, O LORD."
Psalm 70:1-5

RECOLLECTIONS

EXAMEN
PRIDE - ANGER - LUST - ENVY - GREED - GLUTTONY - SLOTH

"Praise the LORD, for he is good: for his mercy endureth for ever.
Praise ye the GOD of gods: for his mercy endureth for ever.
Praise ye the LORD of lords: for his mercy endureth for ever.
Who alone doth great wonders: for his mercy endureth for ever.
Who made the heavens in understanding: for his mercy endureth for ever."
Psalm 136:1-5

MEDITATIONS

PRAYER

Mighty God, I thank Thee that Thou art my shield and my strength. Thou hast promised that all who are weary and burdened, should come to Thee, and Thou will give rest. I ask that Thou givest me rest this evening. May the word of Christ dwell in me richly, teaching me in all wisdom, and producing holiness in my heart that I may glorify Thee in my life. May I sleep with gratitude in my heart to God.
AMEN

APPENDIX

CATHOLICS CREEDS
- Apostles'
- Nicene
- Athanasian
- Chalcedonian
- Tridentine

PRAYER
- Sources of Prayer
- Levels of Prayer

STATE OF GRACE DOCTRINE
- Scriptural Basis
- Doctrine & Dogmas

CHRISTIAN MORALS: FORMATION OF CONSCIENCE
- Ten Commandments
- Church Expositions
- Sins Against Faith
- Sins Against Hope
- Sins Against Charity
- Sins Against Unity
- Mortal Sin
- Seven Deadly Sins Exposition
- Sins of the Senses
- Sins of the Flesh
- Sins of the Tongue
- Sins of the Mind
- Interpersonal Sin
- Accessory to Sin

CONFESSIONAL GUIDE
- Examination of Conscience
- Sacrament of Reconciliation
- Penance

AMENDMENT OF LIFE
- Detecting Predominant Faults
- Remedies for Predominant Faults
- Avoiding Near Occaisions of Sin
- Proactive Deliverance Prayers
- Reactive Deliverance Prayers
- Invocation of Saints

REPARATIONS FOR SIN
- Prayer
- Devotions
- Abstinence
- Fasting
- Mortifications
- Almsgiving

GOOD WORKS
- Corporal Works of Mercy
- Spiritual Works of Piety

VIRTURE & VICE
- Theological Virtues
- Cardinal Virtues and Opposing Vices

STAGES OF SANCTIFICATION
- Purgative State
- Illuminative State
- Unitive State

CATHOLIC CREEDS

THE APOSTLES' CREED

(Est. 341 - 5th CE, A.D.)

I believe in **GOD THE FATHER** Almighty,
Creator of heaven and earth.

And in **JESUS CHRIST** His only Son our Lord;
Who was conceived by the Holy Spirit,
born of the Virgin Mary,
suffered under Pontius Pilate,
was crucified, died, and was buried;
He descended into hell;
On the third day He rose again from the dead;
He ascended into heaven,
and sitteth at the right Hand of God the Father Almighty;
From thence He shall come to judge the living and the dead.

I believe in **THE HOLY SPIRIT**;
the Holy Catholic Church;
the communion of saints;
the forgiveness of sins;
the resurrection of the body;
and life everlasting.

AMEN

<u>**Exclusion of Heretical Movements**</u> (Implicit in the Apostles' Creed):

Docetism - Rejection of the humanity of Jesus, and the bodily resurrection of Christ.

Ebionism & Adoptionism - Rejection of Christ's Miraculous Conception by the Holy Ghost; the Virginity of the Blessed Virgin Mary at the time of the Miraculous Conception; and Mary's role as *'Mother of God'*.

Gnosticism - Rejection of Christ's crucifixion, bodily death and burial. Also rejection of the resurrection of the body.

Modalism - Rejection of the distinctness of the Divine Persons of the Holy Trinity.

All Heretical Factions - Rejection of the Holy Catholic Church and the communion of saints.

THE NICENE CREED

(Est. 381 A.D.)

I believe in one **GOD, THE FATHER** almighty,
maker of heaven and earth, of all things visible & invisible.

I believe in one **LORD JESUS CHRIST**,
the Only Begotten Son of God, born of the Father before all ages.
God from God, Light from Light, true God from true God, begotten, not
made, consubstantial with the Father; through him all things were made.
For us men and for our salvation he came down from heaven,
and by the Holy Spirit was incarnate of the Virgin Mary, and became man.
For our sake he was crucified under Pontius Pilate, he suffered death,
was buried, and rose again on the third day in accordance with the
Scriptures. He ascended into heaven and is seated at the right
hand of the Father. He will come again in glory to judge the living
and the dead and his kingdom will have no end.

I believe in **THE HOLY SPIRIT**, the Lord, the giver of life,
who proceeds from the Father and the Son, who with the Father
and the Son is adored and glorified, who has spoken through the prophets.
I believe in one, Holy, Catholic and Apostolic Church.
I confess one baptism for the forgiveness of sins and I look forward
to the resurrection of the dead and the life of the world to come.
AMEN

Exclusion of Heretical Movements (Implicit in the Nicene Creed):

Polytheism - The belief in the existence of a plurality of Gods. Rejects monotheism.

Panentheism - Rejects that Almighty God is strictly transcendent over creation.

Tritheism - Rejection of the inseparable unity of the Holy Trinity, positing that the
Father, Son and Holy Spirit are three Gods, and not one.

Modalism - Rejection of the distinctness of the Divine Persons of the Holy Trinity.

Docetism - Rejection of the humanity of Jesus, the Incarnation of Christ (The Word
of God), and the bodily resurrection of Christ.

Arianism - Rejection of the Divinity of Jesus Christ as a person of the Holy Trinity,
existing before time; of Christ's Miraculous Conception by the Holy Ghost (in
time); the Virginity of the Blessed Virgin Mary at the time of the Miraculous
Conception; and Mary's role as *'Mother of God'*.

Gnosticism - Rejection of Christ's crucifixion, bodily death and burial. Also
rejection of the resurrection of the body.

Montanists & Catharists - Rejection of one baptism for the forgiveness of sins.
These groups advocated for multiple baptisms.

All Heretical Factions - Rejection of the one, Holy, Catholic, Apostolic Church.

THE ATHANASIAN CREED

(Est. 5th CE, A.D.)

Whoever wishes to be saved must, above all, keep the Catholic faith.
For unless a person keeps this faith whole and entire
he will undoubtedly be lost forever.
This is what the Catholic faith teaches: we worship one God in the Trinity
and the Trinity in unity. We distinguish among the persons,
but we do not divide the substance. For **THE FATHER** is a distinct person;
THE SON is a distinct person; and **THE HOLY SPIRIT** is a distinct person.
Still the Father and the Son and the Holy Spirit have
one divinity, equal glory, and coeternal majesty.
What the Father is, the Son is, and the Holy Spirit is. The Father is
uncreated, the Son is uncreated, and the Holy Spirit is uncreated.
The Father is boundless, the Son is boundless, and the Holy Spirit
is boundless. The Father is eternal, the Son is eternal,
and the Holy Spirit is eternal.
Nevertheless, there are not three eternal beings, but one eternal being.
Thus there are not three uncreated beings, nor three boundless beings,
but one uncreated being and one boundless being.
Likewise, the Father is omnipotent, the Son is omnipotent,
and the Holy Spirit is omnipotent. Yet there are not
three omnipotent beings, but one omnipotent being.
Thus the Father is God, the Son is God, and the Holy Spirit is God.
But there are not three gods, but one God. The Father is Lord,
the Son is Lord, and the Holy Spirit is Lord.
There are not three lords, but one Lord. For according to Christian truth,
we must profess that each of the persons individually is God;
and according to Christian religion we are forbidden
to say that there are three gods or lords.
The Father is not made by anyone, nor created by anyone, nor generated
by anyone. The Son is not made nor created, but he is generated by the
Father alone. The Holy Spirit is not made nor created nor generated,
but proceeds from the Father and the Son.
There is, then, one Father, not three Fathers; one Son, but not three sons;
one Holy Spirit, not three holy spirits. In this Trinity, there is nothing
greater, nothing less than anything else. But the entire three persons are
coeternal and coequal with one another. So that, as we have said,
we worship complete unity in the Trinity and the Trinity in unity.

This, then, is what he who wishes to be saved must believe about the
Trinity. It is also necessary for eternal salvation that he believes
steadfastly in the incarnation of our Lord Jesus Christ.

The true faith is: we believe and profess that our Lord Jesus Christ, the Son of God, is both God and man. As God He was begotten of the substance of the Father before time; as man He was born in time of the substance of His Mother. He is perfect God; and He is perfect man, with a rational soul and human flesh. He is equal to the Father in His divinity, but He is inferior to the Father in His humanity. Although He is God and man, He is not two, but one Christ. And He is one, not because His divinity was changed into flesh, but because His humanity was assumed to God. He is one, not at all because of a mingling of substances, but because He is one person.
As a rational soul and flesh are one man: so God and man are one Christ. He died for our salvation, descended to hell, arose from the dead on the third day. Ascended into heaven, sits at the right hand of God the Father almighty, and from there He shall come to judge the living and the dead. At His coming, all men are to arise with their own bodies; and they are to give an account of their lives. Those who have done good deeds will go into eternal life; those who have done evil will go into everlasting fire.

This is the Catholic faith. Everyone must believe it,
firmly and steadfastly; otherwise He cannot be saved.

AMEN

<u>Exclusion of Heretical Movements</u> (Implicit in the Athanasian Creed):

Polytheism - The belief in the existence of a plurality of Gods. Rejects monotheism.

Panentheism - Rejects that Almighty God is strictly transcendent over creation.

Tritheism - Rejection of the inseparable unity of the Holy Trinity, positing that the Father, Son and Holy Spirit are three Gods, and not one.

Modalism & Sabellianism - Rejection of the distinctness of the Divine Persons of the Holy Trinity.

Monarchianism - Rejects the equality of all Three Persons of the Holy Trinity, rather, affirming God the Father is emphasized as supreme within the Trinity.

Docetism - Rejection of the humanity of Jesus, the Incarnation of Christ (The Word of God), and the bodily resurrection of Christ.

Arianism - Rejection of the Divinity of the Son of God as a person of the Holy Trinity, existing before time; of Christ's Miraculous Conception by the Holy Ghost (in time); the Virginity of the Blessed Virgin Mary at the time of the Miraculous Conception; and Mary's role as *'Mother of God'*.

Appolinarianism - Rejects that Christ has both a human and divine soul & mind.

Nestorianism - Rejects the unity between the divine and human natures of Christ.

All Heretical Factions - Rejection of the Catholic Faith.

CHALCEDONIAN CREED

(Est. 451 A.D.)

We, then, following the holy fathers, all with one consent teach men
to confess one and the same Son, our **LORD JESUS CHRIST**, the same perfect
in Godhead and also perfect in manhood; truly God and truly man,
of a rational soul and body; coessential with **THE FATHER** according to the
Godhead, and consubstantial with us according to the manhood;
in all things like unto us, without sin; begotten before all ages of the Father
according to the Godhead, and in these latter days, for us and for
our salvation, born of the Virgin Mary, the mother of God, according to the
manhood; one and the same Christ, Son, Lord, Only-begotten,
to be acknowledged in two natures, without confusion, without change,
without division, without separation; the distinction of natures being by no
means taken away by the union, but rather the property of each nature
being preserved, and concurring in one person and one subsistence,
not parted or divided into two persons, but one and the same Son,
and only begotten, God the Word, the Lord Jesus Christ; as the prophets
from the beginning have declared concerning Him, and the
Lord Jesus Christ Himself has taught us, and the creed of the
holy fathers has handed down to us.

AMEN

Exclusion of Heretical Movements (Implicit in the Chalcedonian Creed):

Monotheletism - Rejects that Christ has both a human and divine will.

Appolinarianism - Rejects that Christ has both a human and divine soul & mind.

Nestorianism - Rejects the unity between the divine and human natures of Christ.

Modalism & Sabellianism - Rejection of the distinctness of the Divine Persons of
the Holy Trinity.

Docetism - Rejection of the humanity of Jesus, the Incarnation of Christ (The Word
of God), and the bodily resurrection of Christ.

Arianism - Rejection of the Divinity of the Son of God as a person of the Holy
Trinity, existing before time; of Christ's Miraculous Conception by the Holy Ghost
(in time); the Virginity of the Blessed Virgin Mary at the time of the Miraculous
Conception; and Mary's role as *'Mother of God'*.

Monarchianism - Rejects the equality of all Three Persons of the Holy Trinity,
rather, affirming God the Father is emphasized as supreme within the Trinity.

All Heretical Factions - Rejecting Orthodox Christology.

THE TRIDENTINE CREED

(Est. 1565 A.D.)

I, N, with a firm faith believe and profess each and everything which is contained in the Creed which the Holy Roman Church maketh use of.

To wit: I believe in one **GOD, THE FATHER** Almighty, Maker of heaven and earth, and of all things visible and invisible.

And in one **LORD JESUS CHRIST**, the Only-begotten Son of God. Born of the Father before all ages. God of God, Light of Light, true God of true God. Begotten, not made, of one substance with the Father.

By whom all things were made. Who for us men and for our salvation came down from heaven. And became incarnate by the Holy Spirit of the Virgin Mary: and was made man. He was also crucified for us, suffered under Pontius Pilate, and was buried. And on the third day He rose again according to the Scriptures. He ascended into heaven and sits at the right hand of the Father. He will come again in glory to judge the living and the dead and His kingdom will have no end.

I believe in **THE HOLY SPIRIT**, the Lord and Giver of life, Who proceeds from the Father and the Son. Who together with the Father and the Son is adored and glorified, and who spoke through the prophets. And one holy, Catholic and Apostolic Church. I confess one baptism for the forgiveness of sins and I await the resurrection of the dead and the life of the world to come. Amen.

I most steadfastly admit and embrace Apostolical and ecclesiastical traditions, and all other observances and constitutions of the Church. I also admit the Holy Scripture according to that sense which our holy mother the Church hath held, and doth hold, to whom it belongeth to judge of the true sense and interpretations of the Scriptures. Neither will I ever take and interpret them otherwise than according to the unanimous consent of the Fathers.

I also profess that there are truly and properly Seven Sacraments of the New Law, instituted by Jesus Christ our Lord, and necessary for the salvation of mankind, though not all for every one; to wit, Baptism, Confirmation, Eucharist, Penance, Extreme Unction, Holy Orders, and Matrimony; and that they confer grace; and that of these, Baptism, Confirmation, and Holy Orders cannot be reiterated without sacrilege.

I also receive and admit the received and approved ceremonies of the Catholic Church in the solemn administration of the aforesaid sacraments.

I embrace and receive all and every one of the things which have been defined and declared in the holy Council of Trent concerning original sin and justification.

I profess, likewise, that in the Mass there is offered to God a true, proper, and propitiatory sacrifice for the living and the dead; and that in the most holy sacrament of the Eucharist there is truly, really, and substantially, the Body and Blood, together with the soul and divinity, of our Lord Jesus Christ; and that there is made a conversion of the whole substance of the bread into the Body, and of the whole substance of the wine into the Blood, which conversion the Catholic Church calls *Transubstantiation.* I also confess that under either kind alone Christ is received whole and entire, and a true sacrament.

I constantly hold that there is a Purgatory, and that the souls therein detained are helped by the suffrages of the faithful. Likewise, that the saints, reigning together with Christ, are to be honored and invoked, and that they offer prayers to God for us, and that their relics are to be venerated.

I most firmly assert that the images of Christ, of the Mother of God, ever virgin, and also of other Saints, ought to be had and retained, and that due honor and veneration is to be given them.

I also affirm that the power of indulgences was left by Christ in the Church, and that the use of them is most wholesome to Christian people.

I acknowledge the Holy Catholic Apostolic Roman Church as the mother and mistress of all churches; and I promise true obedience to the Bishop of Rome, successor to St. Peter, Prince of the Apostles, and Vicar of Jesus Christ.

I likewise undoubtedly receive and profess all other things delivered, defined, and declared by the sacred Canons, and general Councils, and particularly by the holy Council of Trent, and by the ecumenical Council of the Vatican, particularly concerning the primacy of the Roman Pontiff and his infallible teaching.

I condemn, reject, and anathematize all things contrary thereto, and all heresies which the Church hath condemned, rejected, and anathematized.

This true Catholic faith, outside of which no one can be saved, which I now freely profess and to which I truly adhere, inviolate and with firm constancy until the last breath of life, I do so profess and swear to maintain with the help of God. And I shall strive, as far as possible, that this same faith shall be held, taught, and professed by all those over whom I have charge.

I, N., do so pledge, promise, and swear, so help me God and these Holy Gospels.

AMEN

<u>**Exclusion of Heretical Movements**</u> (Implicit in the Tridentine Creed):

Polytheism - The belief in the existence of a plurality of Gods. Rejects monotheism.

Panentheism - Rejects that Almighty God is transcendent over creation.

Tritheism - Rejection of the inseparable unity of the Holy Trinity, positing that the Father, Son and Holy Spirit are three Gods, and not one.

Modalism & Sabellianism - Rejection of the distinctness of the Divine Persons of the Holy Trinity.

Ebionism & Adoptionism - Rejection of Christ's Miraculous Conception by the Holy Ghost; the Virginity of the Blessed Virgin Mary at the time of the Miraculous Conception; and Mary's role as *'Mother of God'*.

Docetism - Rejection of the humanity of Jesus, the Incarnation of Christ (The Word of God), and the bodily resurrection of Christ.

Arianism - Rejection of the Divinity of Jesus Christ as a person of the Holy Trinity, existing before time; of Christ's Miraculous Conception by the Holy Ghost (in time); the Virginity of the Blessed Virgin Mary at the time of the Miraculous Conception; and Mary's role as *'Mother of God'*.

Gnosticism - Rejection of Christ's crucifixion, bodily death and burial. Also rejection of the resurrection of the body.

Montanists & Catharists - Rejection of one baptism for the forgiveness of sins. These groups advocated for multiple baptisms.

Iconoclasm - Rejection and destruction of Sacred images of saints, angels and the B.V.M., deeming the veneration of such imagery to be heretical.

Protestantism - Rejection of Apostolical and Ecclesiastical Traditions as well as practices in the constitutions of the Church. Rejection of the Church's Authority in the interpretation of Sacred Scripture over and above Her individual members. Rejection of the Sacramental System of the New Law, in full or in part; rejecting that Christ instituted the New Sacramental System. A rejection of the Sacrificial nature of the Mass. Rejection of the Real Presence of Christ in the Holy Eucharist viz. *Transubstantiation.* A rejection of the rites and rituals of the Catholic Church. Rejection of Church doctrine on justification, original sin and other soteriological doctrines. Rejection of the Church teaching on Purgatory, prayer for the dead, and expiation for those in purgatory. Rejection of the legitimacy, power and practice of Indulgences. Rejection of the supremacy of the Holy, Roman Catholic, Apostolic, Church and the Bishop of Rome as successor of St. Peter, Prince of the Apostles, Vicar of Christ; thus, a rejection of the Papacy and Episcopacy - of Jesus Christ's institution of It. Rejections of any single teachings of the Ecumenical Councils held in Church History, and the *Ex Cathedra* teachings of the Popes. The practical rejection of Ecclesiastical Unity.

All Heretical Factions - Rejection of the one, Holy, Catholic, Apostolic Church, Her structure, constitution, supreme authority and any of Her dogmas, ritual practices, canons and conciliar declarations.

PRAYER

"The lifting of the mind & heart [the will] to God —
to engage in conversation with the Almighty."

SOURCES OF PRAYER

Scripture - The Church - Public Revelation
- Private Revelation - Spontaneous

TYPES & LEVELS OF PRAYER

"There is a direct correlation between where one is in their spiritual life (virtue)
and how developed one is in terms of these 9-Levels of Prayer." - **Fr. C. Ripperger**

Vocal (Public & Private) - Recitation of formulated prayers, requiring devotion & attention. *Ex. Mass, Liturgy of the Hours, Breviary etc.*

Mental - Meditation on theological realities, involving the imagination. The consideration of theological realities from various points-of-view.
Ex. The Holy Trinity, Creation, The Fall, Biblical History, The Covenants, Lord Jesus Christ, The Redemption, The Church, The Priesthood, The Sacraments, Vice & Virtue, Heaven, Hell, Purgatory etc.

Effective - Operations of the will predominate over the intellect in producing Acts of Love towards God, leading to the purification of intentions. *Ex. Deliverance Prayers, Renunciation of Evils etc.*

Prayer of Simplicity - All faculties fix their concentration on a single theological object, yielding an intense focus.

Active Purgation - All things done in cooperation with ordinary graces in order to dispose the will to serving God — the active rooting out of personal vices & evils.

Contemplative / Mystical - The infusion or invasion of the Soul by the Supernatural. An experiential knowledge of God occurring passively.

Prayer of Quiet - Infused contemplation which principally involves the intellect (which is withdrawn from the other faculties), and the will.

Illuminative - God communicates truths to the Soul, impossible to know otherwise, through supernatural infusion.

Unitive - God totally captivates all faculties of the Soul which becomes divinized, so to speak, by God. The Soul experiences a state of ecstasy, when recognizing God in her, and her in God. The Soul comes to a transforming union, being conformed in likeness to God.

STATE OF GRACE DOCTRINE

JESUS
"If you love me, keep my commandments... He that hath my
commandments, and keepeth them; he it is that loveth me."
Jn 14:15, 21

"And he that loveth me, shall be loved of my Father: and I will love
him, and will manifest myself to him... If any one love me,
he will keep my word, and my Father will love him,
and we will come to him, and will make our abode with him.
He that loveth me not, keepeth not my words."
Jn 14:21, 23-24

"I AM the True Vine;
and my Father is the Husbandman.
Every branch in me, that beareth not fruit, he will take
away: and every one that beareth fruit, he will purge it,
that it may bring forth more fruit.
Now you are clean by reason of the word, which I have spoken to
you. Abide in me, and I in you. As the branch cannot bear fruit of
itself, unless it abide in the vine, so neither can you, unless you
abide in me. I AM the Vine; you the branches: he that abideth in me,
and I in him, the same beareth much fruit: for without me you can
do nothing. If any one abide not in me, he shall be cast forth as a
branch, and shall wither, and they shall gather him up, and cast him
into the fire, and he burneth. If you abide in me, and my words
abide in you, you shall ask whatever you will,
and it shall be done unto you.
In this is my Father glorified; that you bring forth very much fruit,
and become my disciples. As the Father hath loved me, I also have
loved you. Abide in my love. If you keep my commandments,
you shall abide in my love; as I also have kept my Father's
commandments, and do abide in his love. These things I have
spoken to you, that my joy may be in you, and your joy may be
filled. This is my commandment, that you love one another,
as I have loved you."
Jn 15:1-10

Definitions:

GRACE - A supernatural help of God granted in consideration of the merits of Christ (The Passion, Vicarious Atonement *etc*).

JUSTIFICATION - Justification as an act, is the work of God alone, presupposing, on the part of the recipient, the process of justification and the cooperation of his free will with God's grace.

SANCTIFYING GRACE - A supernatural gift of God to intellectual creatures (men, angels) for their eternal salvation, whether the latter be furthered and attained through salutary acts or a state of holiness.

STATE OF GRACE (STATE OF JUSTIFICATION) - The condition of a person (and their soul) who is free from mortal sin and pleasing to God. Also, the state of being in God's friendship. The State of Grace is an absolutely necessary condition of the soul at death, in order to attain eternal life in heaven.

"Those who through sin have forfeited the grace of justification they had received can be justified again [can. 29] when, awakened by God, they make the effort to regain through the sacrament of penance and by the merits of Christ, the grace which they have lost.
This manner of justification is the restoration of the sinner that the holy Fathers aptly call "the second plank {of salvation} after the shipwreck of lost grace". For Christ Jesus instituted the sacrament of penance for those who fall into sin after baptism, when he said: "Receive the Holy Spirit; whose sins you shall forgive, they are forgiven, and whose sins you shall retain, they are retained" [Jn 20:22].
Hence it must be taught that the repentance of a Christian after his fall into sin differs vastly from repentance at the time of baptism. It includes not only giving up sins and detesting them, or "a broken and contrite heart" [Ps 51:17], but also their sacramental confession, (or at least their desire to confess them when a suitable occasion will be found) and the absolution of a priest… For the eternal punishment… together with the guilt, is remitted by the reception or the desire of the sacrament."
COUNCIL OF TRENT
(Session VI, c. XIV)

Christians lose salvation by mortal sin and regain it in Sacramental Confession: *"Remember from what you have fallen: do penance, and preform the works you did at first."* [Rev 2:5]

CHRISTIAN MORALS : FORMATION OF CONSCIENCE

*"Blessed is the man who hath not walked in the counsel of the ungodly, nor stood in the way of sinners… But his will is in the Law of the LORD, and on His Law he shall meditate day and night." - **Psalm 1:1-2***

THE TEN COMMANDMENTS

I
THOU SHALT HAVE NO OTHER GODS BEFORE ME

II
THOU SHALT NOT TAKE THE NAME OF THE LORD IN VAIN

III
REMEMBER TO KEEP THE LORD'S DAY HOLY

IV
THOU SHALT HONOR THY FATHER & MOTHER

V
THOU SHALT NOT MURDER

VI
THOU SHALT NOT COMMIT ADULTERY

VII
THOU SHALT NOT STEAL

VIII
THOU SHALT NOT BEAR FALSE WITNESS

IX
THOU SHALT NOT COVET THY NEIGHBOUR'S WIFE

X
THOU SHALT NOT COVET THY NEIGHBOUR'S GOODS

---

*"If thou wilt enter into life, keep the commandments…" - **Mt 19:17***

THE CHURCH EXPOUNDS ON THE COMMANDS

I - THOU SHALT HAVE NO OTHER GODS [OR IDOLS] BEFORE ME

The Lord your God is One. You shall love the Lord with all your heart,
all your mind, all your soul and all your strength. - Mk 12:29

Any & all <u>beliefs</u> contrary to rightly ordered belief in the Holy Trinity as revealed by God:

Atheism - A denial of the existence of God and all of the consequential ideologies which stem from such belief. *Ex. Naturalism, Scientism, Communism etc.*

Paganism / Polytheism - A denial of Monotheism and the belief that there are a plurality of gods. *Ex. Norse Mythology, Roman & Greek Paganism, Hinduism, Indigenous Paganism etc.*

False Monotheism - A rejection of the fully and divinely revealed truths about God in the Old & New Testaments. Rejection of the Holy Trinity: Father, Son and Holy Spirit. *Ex. Judaism, Islam, Taoism etc.*

Religious Indifferentism - Denial that it is the duty of people to worship God by believing and practicing the one true religion.

Apostasy - The abandonment or renunciation of a religious belief or principle.

Heresy - Belief or opinion contrary to true religious doctrine.

Agnosticism - Doubtful or noncommittal attitude towards the existence of God as divinely revealed.

1

SCRIPTURES: Ex 17:2-7; 19:16-25; 20:2-5; 24:15-18. **Deut** 4:15-16; 5:6-9; 6:4-5, 16; 18:10. **Num** 21:4-9. **Jos** 3:10. **1 Kgs** 6:23-28. **Ps** 42:3; 51:17; 95:9. **Jer** 10:1; 29:8. **Is** 1:10-20. **Am** 5:21-25. **Hos** 6:6. **Mt** 4:10; 6:24; 9:13; 10:8-10; 12:7; 22:37; 23:16-22.. **Lk** 1:46-47; 4:8-9; 10:7, 27; 18:1. **Jn** 3:14-15. **Acts** 8:9-24; 18:18; 21:23-24. **Rom** 1:5, 18; 16:26; 18-32. **1 Cor** 9:5-18; 10:9. **Gal** 5:20. **Eph** 5:5. **Heb** 9:13-14. **Rev** 13-14.

CHURCH FATHERS: St. Justin Martyr, *Dial. Cum Tryphone Judaeo, 1:Pg 6*, 497. St. Augustine, *De Civ. Dei 10, 6: Pl 41*, 283. Origen, *Contra Celsum.* St. Basil, *De Spiritu Sancto 18, 45: Pg 32, 149c.* St. Thomas Aquinas, *Summa Theologica II-III, 81, 3 ad 3.*

COUNCILS & CANONS: Council of Nicaea II: DS 601. Council of Trent: DS 1821-1825. Vatican Council II: SC 126; LG 67. CIC, cann.

ENCYCLICALS: Leo XIII, *Immortale Dei; Libertas Praestantissimum.* Pius XI, *Quas Primas.* Pius XII, *AAS.* Pius VI, *Quod Aliquantum.* Pius IX, *Quanta Cura.*

CATECHISMS: Catechism of the Catholic Church (CCC) Para. 2084 - 2141.
Roman Catechism (RC) 2, 3, 4. Baltimore Catechism Less 30. Spirago Catechism Chp 11.

Materialism - A tendency to consider material possessions and physical comforts as more important than spiritual values.

Omnism - Belief in all religions and religious views as being equally good and true.

Syncretism - The amalgamation, or attempt at amalgamation of different religions, cultures or schools of thought. *Ex. Free Masonry.*

Pantheism - Doctrine identifying God with the universe as a manifestation of God.

Any & all <u>acts</u> against the First Commandment:

Idolatry - Extreme admiration, love and reverence, for someone or something other than God.

Superstition - A vice opposed to religion by way of excess... because it offers Divine worship to beings other than God, or offers worship to God in an improper manner. *Ex. Idolatry, divination, vain or false observances.*

Divination / Magic - The seeking after knowledge of future or hidden things by inadequate means. *Ex. Invocations of spirits &/or nature through signs.*

Blasphemy - Gross irreverence towards God, or any person worth high esteem.

Presumption on God's Mercy - Disordered expectation on the forgiveness of personal sins without truthful & adequate penance.

Despair of God's Mercy - The voluntary and complete abandonment of all hope of saving one's soul and of having the means required for that end.

Neglect of Christian Duties - The condition of not heeding. More specifically it is here considered as the omission, whether habitual or not, of the care required for the performance of duties, or at any rate, for their full, adequate discharge.

He that loveth father or mother more than me, is not worthy of me;
and he that loveth son or daughter more than me,
*is not worthy of me. - **Mt 10:37***

II - THOU SHALT NOT TAKE THE NAME OF THE LORD IN VAIN

For by thy words thou shalt be justified,
and by thy words thou shalt be condemned. - Mt 12:37

Any & all misuse of the Holy Name of God:

Profanation - The act of depriving something sacred of its sacred character.

Irreverence - A lack of respect for people or things generally taken seriously.

Rash Oaths - Taking an oath without careful consideration of the possibilities involved.

False Oaths - An invocation to God to witness the truth of a statement, even though the statement is, in fact, untrue.

Perjury - The crime of taking a false oath.

Criticizing God - Criticism of God &/or the attributes & operations of God, such as, His *Mercy, Justice, Providence etc.*

Neglecting to Correct Members of Household - Failing to admonish or correct family members who misuse the Lord's name in vain.

Blasphemy - Gross irreverence towards God. *Ex. Words of hatred, defiance, reproach etc.*

Idolatry - Extreme admiration, love and reverence, for someone or something other than God. Invoking God's Name improperly *i.e. superstition.*

But I say unto you, that every idle word that men shall speak,
they shall render an account for it in the day of judgment. - Mt 12:36

2

SCRIPTURES: **Ex** 20:7. **Deut** 5:11; 6:13. **Ps** 29:2; 96:2; 113:1-2. **Is** 43:1. **Zech** 2:13. **Mt** 5:33-34; 10:32; 28:19. **Jn** 10:3. **2 Cor** 1:23. **Gal** 1:20. **1 Tim** 6:12. **Jas** 2:7; 5:12. **1 Jn** 1:10. **Rev** 2:17; 14:1.

CHURCH FATHERS: Tertullian, *De Idolatria Chp II.* St. Jerome, *Eustochium De Virg. Serv Ep 22.* St. Augustine, *De serm. Dom. in monte 2, 5, 19: Pl 34,1278; De Civ Dei I Chp 36.* St. John Chrysostom, *Homily on Gospel of St. Matthew.* St. Basil, *Homi de Psalm 33.* St. J. H. Newman, *Parochial and Plain Sermons V, 2: 21-22.*

COUNCILS & CANONS: CIC, cann. 214, 855, 1199, 1369, 1376.

CATECHISMS: C.C.C. Para. 2142 - 2167. Spirago Catechism Chp 12. Baltimore Catechism Less 31. Roman Catechism 3.

Any & all Failures to Honour the Lord's Day:

Unnecessary Transactions - Buying and / or selling of discretionary goods.

Unnecessary Servile Work - Exchanging of services for profit or personal gain.

Demanding Unnecessary Work - Delegating of services for profit or personal gain.

Omission of Worship - Failing to attend worship service, without legitimate cause, when otherwise able to attend.

Irreverent Behaviour at Mass / Service - Lack of due attention, respect, and participation in worship service.

Gambling - Inappropriate gambling / risk-taking behaviour. *Esp. during the designated occasion where spiritual thoughts, conversations and actions ought to be prioritized.*

Insobriety - Inappropriate level of intoxication from overconsumption of alcohol.

Slothfulness / Idleness - Laziness. State of inaction / inactivity.

Negligence of Christian Duties - Neglecting to advance individual or familial theological virtues (*faith, hope, love*) and other virtues in general (*prudence, temperance, justice, fortitude*).

Accessory to Sin Against the 3rd Command - Allowing, consenting, participation, encouraging, delegating, provoking, commanding or coercing someone to sin.

The Son of man is Lord even of the sabbath. - ***Mt 12:8***
Therefore it is lawful to do a good deed on the sabbath days. - ***Mt 12:12***

3

SCRIPTURES: Gen 2:2. **Ex** 20:8-11; 23:12; 31:15-17. **Deut** 5:12-15. **Neh** 13:15-22. **2 Chr** 36:21. **Ps** 118:24. **Mt** 12:5; 16:2; 28:1. **Mk** 1:21; 2:27-28; 3:4; 16:1-2. **Lk** 24:1. **Jn** 7:23; 9:16; 20:1. **1 Cor** 10:11, 17. **Heb** 10:25; 12:22-23. **Acts** 2:42-46.

CHURCH FATHERS: St. Ignatius of Antioch, *Ad Magn. 9, 1: Sch 10, 88*. St. Justin, *I Apol. 67*: Pg 6, 429, 432. St. John Chrysostom, *De incomprehensibili 3, 6*: Pg 48, 725. St. Augustine, *De civ. Dei 19, 19*: Pl 41, 647. St. Thomas Aquinas, *STh II-III, 122, 4*.

COUNCILS & CANONS: CIC, cann. 515, 1245, 1246, 1247, 1248.

CATECHISM: C.C.C. Paras. 2168 - 2195.

IV - THOU SHALT HONOR THY FATHER & MOTHER

FOR CHILDREN, LAITY, CITIZENS, SUBJECTS, STUDENTS, EMPLOYEES

Any & All Failures to Honour Superiors:

Disobedience - Failure or refusal to obey established rules &/or someone in authority.

Disrespect of Superiors & their Possessions - Lack of respect for individuals in place of authority &/or for their possessions.

Neglect of Due Honour - Failing to care for demonstrating proper honour to individuals in positions of authority.

Neglect of the Elderly - Failing to care for, attend to, and supply with necessities, those of advanced age in one's family, community etc.

Refusal to Speak to Superiors - Scornful silence towards those in authority over oneself.

Resentment of Superiors - Bitter indignation towards ones superiors.

Disobedience to Civil Laws - The breaking of civil laws, established for the benefit of the community.

4

SCRIPTURES: Ex 20:12. **Deut** 5:16; 6:4-5. **Lev** 19:18. **Isa** 58:6-7. **Dan** 3:79-81. **Am** 8:4-6. **Prov** 6:20-22; 13:1; 17:6. **Sir** 3:12-13. 7:27-28; 30:1-2. **Mt** 10: 37; 12: 49; 16:25; 18:21-22; 22:21, 34-40. **Mk** 7:8-13; 12:29-31. **Lk** 2:51; 10:25-28; 17:4. **Jn** 12:8. **Acts** 5:29. **2 Cor** 8:9. **Jas** 1:27. **Eph** 3:14; 4:2; 5:21-6; 6:1-4. **1 Pet** 2:13; 3:1-7. **1 Jn** 13:34. **Rom** 13:1-2, 7-10. **Col** 3:20. **1Tim** 2:2. **2 Tim** 1:5.

CHURCH FATHERS: Ad Diognetum 5, 5 and 10; 6, 10: Pg 2, 1173 and 1176.

ENCYCLICALS & CANONS: St. Gregory the Great, *Regula Pastoralis.* 3, 21: PL 77, 87.

CATECHISM: C.C.C. Paras. 2197 - 2257.

IV - *Continued...*

Any & All Failures of Duty Towards Subordinates:

Failure to Lead by Good Example - Neglect in demonstrating virtue, good will and good character in leadership.

Failure to Admonish & Correct - Omitting constructive warning and correction of those one is responsible for.

Harsh Criticism - Destructive criticisms causing negative outcomes.

Failure to Protect Them From Harms - Neglecting to protect dependants as necessary.

Failure to Honour Subordinates - Omitting to give due honour, respect and fair treatment to dependants.

Failure to Educate & Train - Neglecting to provide or ensure sound education and training of dependents.

Failure to Provide Physical & Spiritual Necessities - Neglecting to provide the basic necessities of life and basic spiritual necessities for the well-being of dependents.

V - THOU SHALT NOT MURDER

*You have heard that it was said to them of old: Thou shalt not kill. And whosoever shall kill shall be in danger of the judgment. But I say to you, that whosoever is angry with his brother, shall be in danger of the judgment. - **Mt 5:21-22***

Contempt - The feeling that a person is beneath consideration, worthless, or deserving scorn.

Hatred - Intense dislike or ill-will towards someone or something.

Contumely / Derision - Abusive language or treatment of someone. *Insults, slander, slurs, derision, invective, disparagement. Mockery.*

Detraction - The unjust damaging of another's reputation by speaking of some fault or crime of which that other is really guilty, or at any rate, is seriously believed to be guilty, by the defamer.

Defamation / Calumny - The action of damaging the reputation of another, esp. with false information.

Racism - Prejudice, discrimination or antagonism against a person or people on the basis of their membership in a specific racial or ethnic group.

Sedition - Conduct or speech inciting people to rebel against the authority of the state or monarch.

Treason - The crime of betraying one's country.

Terrorism - The unlawful use of violence and intimidation against civilians, in the pursuit of political gains.

Contraception - The deliberate use of artificial means to prevent conception as a consequence of sexual intercourse.

Suicide - The action of killing oneself intentionally.

Murder - The unlawful, premeditated killing of one person by another.

Abortion - The deliberate termination of a human pregnancy.

Onanism - Spilling of the male seed. *Coitus interruptus.*

Genocide - The deliberate killing of a large group of people from a particular nation or ethnic group with the aim of destroying that group.

5

SCRIPTURE: Gen 4:8-12; 9:5-6. **Ex** 20:13; 23:7. **Deut** 5:17. **Lev** 17:14. **Job** 10:8-12. **Ps** 22:10-11; 139:15. **Is** 9:5; 32:17. **Am** 8:4-10. **Mt** 5:21-39, 44-45; 7:15; 18:6; 26:52. **Lk** 17:1; 23:40-43. **1 Cor** 8:10-13. **Col** 1:20-22. 3:21. **Eph** 2:14-16.

CHURCH FATHERS: *Didache* 2, 2: SCh 248, 148. Tertullian, *Apol.* 9:Pl 1, 319-320. St. Augustine, *De civ Dei*, 19, 13, 1: PL 41, 640. St. Thomas Aquinas, *STh* II-II, 64, 7, *corp. art.*

ENCYCLICALS & CANONS: John Paul II, *Evangelium vitae 56.* CDF, *Donum vitae* I, 1, 3, 5-6; III. CIC, cann. 1176, 1314, 1323 - 1324, 1398. Pius XII, *Discourse,* June 1, 1941.

VI - THOU SHALT NOT COMMIT ADULTERY

*You have heard that it was said to them of old: Thou shalt not commit adultery.
But I say to you, that whosoever shall look on a woman to lust after her,
hath already committed adultery with her in his heart. - **Mt 5:27-28***

Lustful Looks - Looking at someone with the express intention of deriving sexual pleasure from their appearance.

Double Takes - Looking at someone multiple times in order to derive sexual pleasure.

Pornography - Printed or visual material containing the explicit description or display of sexual organs or sexual activity, intended to stimulate erotic, rather than aesthetic or emotional feelings.

Lustful Delectations - Engaging disordered sexual thoughts for pleasure and delight. *Ex. Fantasizing, impure reading material.*

Covetousness - Having a great desire of possessing something or someone belonging to or in an established relationship with another.

Masturbation - Self-stimulation of reproductive organs for sexual pleasure.

Onanism - Spilling of the male seed. *Coitus interruptus.*

Seduction - Tempting another towards sexual attraction.

Fornication - Sexual intercourse between unmarried individuals.

Adultery - Voluntary sexual intercourse between a married person and a person other than their spouse.

Sodomy - Sexual intercourse involving anal or oral copulation… *Esp. in same-sex intercourse.*

Incest - Sexual relations between people classed too closely related to marry one another.

Rape - The crime of forcing another person to have sexual intercourse against their will.

6

SCRIPTURE: Gen 1:27-28; 2:24; 4:1-2; 5:1-2; 15:2; 19:1-29; 30:1. **Ex** 20:14. **Deut** 5:18. **Lev** 18:7-20. **Tob** 8:4-9. **Hos** 2:7. **Jer** 5:7; 13:27. **Mt** 5:27-28, 37; 19:1-12; 23:9. **Mk** 10:9-11. **Lk** 16:18. **Jn** 15:15. **1 Jn** 3:3. **Titu** 2:1-6. **Gal** 3:27. **Eph** 3:14. **1 Cor** 5:1. 6:15-20; 7:10-11. **Rom** 1:24-27. **1 Tim** 1:10.

CHURCH FATHERS: St. Ambrose, *De Viduis* 4, 23:Pl 16, 255A. St. Augustine, *Conf.* 10, 29, 40: Pl 32, 796. St. John Chrysostom, *Hom. In Eph* 20, 8: Pg 62, 146-147. St. Basil, *Moralia* 73, 1: Pg 31, 849-852.

ENCYCLICALS & CANONS: CDF, *Persona humana* 7, 8, 9, 11; *Domnum vitae* II: 1, 2, 4, 5, 8. Pius XII, *Discourse*, Oct. 29, 1951. CIC, cann. 1056, 1151-1156. Pius XI, *Casti connubii.* HV 11-12, 14, 16.

Theft / Robbery - The action/crime of stealing what belongs to others.

Time-Theft - Stealing paid time in the workplace. *Ex. Taking longer breaks, extending clock-out time.*

Bribing / Grafting - Persuading someone to act in your favour by gift of money or some other benefit.

Cheating - Dishonest actions in order to gain advantages over others.

Vandalism - Actions involving the deliberate destruction or damaging of public or private property.

False Weights & Measures - False labeling/descriptions of goods sold by merchants.

False Brokering - Persuasion of others to make unsound investments with the assurance of gain.

Counterfeiting - Fabrications done in order to imitate something of value, with the intention to deceive or defraud.

Unjust Wages - When employers pay their employees disproportionately low wages compared to the work performed.

Defrauding Labourers - When employers deliberately deceive employees in order to retain more revenues or gain some advantage.

Failure to Pay Back Debts - Defaulting on or neglecting to pay monetary debts owed to the creditor.

Failure to Pay Bills - Omitting to pay for regular financial obligations.

Depriving Dependants - Detracting from the physical/financial necessities of dependants due to reckless behaviours. *Ex. Gambling, drinking, foolish spending.*

Retaining Stolen Items - Keeping items obtained that you know have been stolen from others.

Failing to Admonish Children - Failing to correct/instruct children of sins against the 7th Commandment.

7

SCRIPTURES: Gen 1:26-31; 2:19-20; 3:14-19; 9:1-4. **Ex** 20:15. **Deut** 5:19; 15:11; 24:15-15; 25:13-16. **Lev** 19:13. **Isa** 58:6-7. **Dan** 3:79-81. **Am** 8:4-6. **Mt** 5:42; 6:2-4, 24-26; 8:20; 19:18; 25:31-46. **Mk** 12:41-44. **Lk** 3:11; 11:41. 16:13; 19:8. **Jn** 12:8. **2 Cor** 8:9. **Jas** 2:15-16; 5:1-6. **Eph** 4:28. **1 Thess** 4:11. **2 Thess** 3:10. **1 Jn** 3:17.

ENCYCLICALS & CANONS: St. Gregory the Great, *Regula Pastoralis.* 3, 21: PL 77, 87. CDF, instruction, *Libertatis conscientia,* 68.

Boasting/Bragging - Excessively proud and self-satisfied talk about one's own achievements, possessions or abilities.

Flattery/Adulation - Excessive and insincere praise, esp. when given to further one's own interests.

Gossip - Casual or unconstrained conversation or reports about other people, typically involving details that are not confirmed as true.

Complaisance - Excessive willingness to please others. *Hyper-agreeableness.*

Lying - Falsification(s) in statements; esp. grave when intended to deceive &/or injure.

Breaking Promises - Failing to keep the secrets that another entrusted you with.

Detraction - The disclosure of another's faults and failings without objectively valid reason.

Defamation/Calumny - The action of damaging another's name and reputation esp. with false and fabricated remarks or claims.

False Oaths - An invocation to God to witness the truth of a statement, even though the statement is, in fact, untrue.

Fraud - Wrongful or criminal deception intended to result in financial or personal gain.

Perjury - The crime of taking a false oath.

Rash Judgements - The assumptions of the moral faults of another without sufficient foundation in alleged accusations.

Hypocrisy - The practice of claiming to have moral standards or beliefs to which one's own behaviour does not conform. *Pretense.*

Sabotage - The deliberate action aimed at destroying or obstructing something.

8

SCRIPTURE: Gen 1:26. **Ex** 20:16. **Deut** 5:20. **Ps** 119:30, 90, 142. **Prov** 8:7; 18:5; 19:9; 25:9-10. **Sam** 7:28. **Sir** 21:28; 27:16. **Wis** 7:16-17, 25-30; 8:2; 13:3, 5. **Mt** 5:33, 37; 18:16. **Lk** 1:50. **Jn** 1:14; 8:12, 32, 44; 12:46; 14:6; 16:13; 17:17; 18:37. **Acts** 24:16. **1 Jn** 1:6. **2 Tim** 1:8. **Col** 2:9. **Eph** 4:24-25. **Heb** 1:3.

CHURCH FATHERS: *Martyrium Polycarpi* 14, 2-3: Pg 5, 1040; SCh 10, 228. St. Ignatius of Antioch, *Ad Rom.* 4, 1: SCh 10,110; Ad Rom. 6, 1-2: SCh 10, 114. St. Augustine, *De mendacio*, 4, 5, : PL 40, 491. St. Thomas Aquinas, *STh* II-II, 109, 3, ad 1. St. Ignatius of Loyola, *Spiritual Exercises*, 22.

ENCYCLICALS & CANONS: CIC, cann. 220, 983. Pius XII, *Musicae sacrae disciplina*; Discourses Sept 3, Dec 25, 1950.

Lustful Looks - Looking at someone with the express intention of deriving sexual pleasure from their appearance.

Double Takes - Looking at someone multiple times in order to derive sexual pleasure.

Pornography - Printed or visual material containing the explicit description or display of sexual organs or sexual activity, intended to stimulate erotic, rather than aesthetic or emotional feelings.

Lustful Delectations - Engaging disordered sexual thoughts for pleasure and delight. *Ex. Fantasizing, impure reading material.*

Covetousness - Having a great desire of possessing something or someone belonging to or in an established relationship with another.

Masturbation - Self-stimulation of reproductive organs for sexual pleasure.

Seduction - Tempting another towards sexual attraction.

Adultery - Voluntary sexual intercourse between a married person and a person other than their spouse.

9

SCRIPTURE: Gen 1:27-28; 2:24; 3:11; 4:1-2; 5:1-2; 15:2; 19:1-29; 30:1. **Ex** 20:14, 17. **Deut** 5:18. **Lev** 18:7-20. **Tob** 8:4-9. **Hos** 2:7. **Jer** 5:7; 13:27. **Mt** 5:8; 27-28, 37; 15:19; 19:1-12; 23:9. **Mk** 10:9-11. **Lk** 16:18. **Jn** 15:15. **1 Jn** 2:16; 3:2-3. **Titu** 2:1-6. **Gal** 3:27; 5:16-17, 24-25. **Eph** 2:3; 3:14. **1 Cor** 5:1. 6:15-20; 7:10-11; 13:12. **Rom** 1:24-27; 12:2. **1 Tim** 1:10; 4:3-9. **2 Tim** 2:23-26. **Titu** 1:15. **1 Thess** 4:7. **Col** 1:10.

CHURCH FATHERS: Pastor Hermae, *Mandate* 2, 1: Pg 2, 916. St. Ambrose, *De Viduis* 4, 23:Pl 16, 255A. St. Augustine, *Conf.* 10, 29, 40: Pl 32, 796; *Conf.* 6, 11, 20: Pl 32, 729-730; St. Augustine, *De fide et symbolo* 10, 25: Pl 40, 196. St. John Chrysostom, *Hom. In Eph* 20, 8: Pg 62, 146-147. St. Basil, *Moralia* 73, 1: Pg 31, 849-852.

COUNCILS, ENCYCLICALS & CANONS: Council of Trent: DS 1515. CDF, *Persona humana* 7, 8, 9, 11; *Domnum Vitae* II: 1, 2, 4, 5, 8. Pius XII, Discourse, Oct. 29, 1951. CIC, cann. 1056, 1151-1156. Pius XI, *Casti connubii*. HV 11-12, 14, 16. St. John Paul II, *DeV* 55.

CATECHISMS: C.C.C. Paras. 2514 - 2533.

X - THOU SHALT NOT COVET THY NEIGHBOUR'S GOODS

Take heed and beware of all covetousness; for a man's life doth not consist in the abundance of thing's which he possesseth - **Lk 12:15**

Ingratitude - A discreditable lack of gratitude.

Covetousness - Having or showing great desire to possess something belonging to another.

Envy - A feeling of discontented or resentful longing aroused by another's possessions, qualities or luck.

Greed - Intense and selfish desire for something, *esp. wealth, power or food.*

Idolatry - Extreme admiration, love and reverence, for someone or something other than God.

Scheming - Given to or involved in making secret and underhanded plans.

Hatred - Intense dislike or ill-will towards someone or something.

Curses - A solemn utterance intended to invoke supernatural power to inflict harm or punishment on someone or something.

Lust - Strongly disordered sexual desire for someone or something.

Sabotage - The deliberate action aimed at destroying or obstructing something.

Sadism - The tendency to derive pleasure from inflicting pain, suffering or humiliation on others.

Overwhelming Ambition - A strongly disordered desire to do or achieve something.

For where thy treasure is, there thy heart is also - **Mt 6:21**

10

SCRIPTURE: **Gen** 3:6; 4:3-7. **Ex** 20:17. **Deut** 5:21. **Lev** 26:12. **Wis** 2:24; 14:12. **Sir** 5:8. **2 Sam** 12:1-4. **1 Kgs** 21:1-29. **Mic** 2:2. **Mt** 5:3; 6:21, 25-34. **Mk** 8:35. **Lk** 6:20, 24; 14:33; 21:4. **Rom** 3:21-22; 7:7; 23; 8:14, 27. **1 Cor** 15:28. **2 Cor** 8:9, 27, 2-4. **Gal** 5:24. **1 Jn** 2:16. **Rev** 22:17.

CHURCH FATHERS: St. John Chrysostom, *Hom. in 2 Cor.*, 3-4: Pg 61, 588; *Hom. In Rom.* 71, 5: PG 60, 448. St. Augustine, *De catechizandis rudibus* 4, 8: PL 40, 315-316. St. Gregory of Nyssa, *De beatitudinibus* 6: Pg 44, 1265A. St. Gregory the Great, *Moralis in Job* 31, 45: PL 76, 621.

CATECHISMS: C.C.C. Paras. 2534 - 2557. Roman Catechism III, 37.

SIN

CHATÁ (Hebrew) - HAMARTIA (Greek) - PECCATUM (Latin)
MISSING THE MARK / OFF THE MARK

Definitions:

EVIL - **(A)** A privation of form, order or due measure. **(B)** A deficiency in perfection.
METAPHYSICAL EVIL - **(A)** The negation of a greater good. **(B)** The limitation of finite beings by other finite beings.
PHYSICAL EVIL - Deprives affected subjects of some natural good, and is adverse to the well-being of the subject, as pain and suffering.
MORAL EVIL - A deprivation of moral good. Found only in intelligent beings.
SIN - A moral evil.

MORTAL SIN (DEADLY, GRAVE, SERIOUS)

Three Essential Components:

1. GRAVE MATTER - Any desire, belief, thought, word, or deed contrary to Eternal Law.
2. FULL KNOWLEDGE - Conscious awareness of the established Law / Moral order.
    *** Ignorance** - *Lack of knowledge about a thing in a being capable of knowing.*
3. VOLUNTARY / DELIBERATE - A free act proceeding from the will with the apprehension of the end sought.

Absolute Exceptions:

***INVINCIBLE IGNORANCE** - A state of ignorance impossible of reversing.

SEVEN DEADLY SINS (CAPITAL VICES)

PRIDE - The excessive love of one's own excellence.
ANGER - The desire of vengeance.
LUST - The disordered desire, or indulgence, of carnal / sexual pleasure.
ENVY - A sorrow which one entertains at another's well-being due to the view that one's own excellence is lessened by consequence.
GREED - The inordinate desire for riches, & / or love of them.
GLUTTONY - The excessive desire for & / or indulgence in food & drink.
SLOTH - Disinclination to labour or exertion.

Sources of Temptation

THE WORLD - The temporal realm consisting of continents, nations, societies / civilizations, cities, towns, and villages, with all of their temporal movements— sociocultural currents and changes etc.
THE FLESH - The lower faculties of human beings— Libido, passions, instincts & impulses.
THE DEVIL - Satan and his demons.

Common Interior Dispositions of Sin

MALICE - The intention or desire to do evil. *Ill will.*
HUMAN RESPECTS - Acting to satisfy social motives over moral / spiritual ones.
WEAKNESS - The state or condition of lacking strength— in moral / spiritual matters.
IGNORANCE - Lack of knowledge or information— in moral matters.

SINS AGAINST FAITH

- Unbelief
- Heresy
- Apostasy

SINS AGAINST HOPE

Despair - The voluntary and complete abandonment of all hope of saving one's soul and of having the means required for that end.

SINS AGAINST CHARITY

- Any & All Sins Against the Ten Commandments.
- Any & All Grave Sins Against the Moral Teachings of the Church

SINS AGAINST UNITY

Strife - Angry or bitter disagreement over fundamental issues.

Factionalism - Dissent and fragmentation of a group into sub-groups.

Heresy - Belief or opinion contrary to true religious dogma & doctrine.

Apostasy - The abandonment or renunciation of a religious belief or principle.

Schism - The rupture of ecclesiastical union / unity. The practical denial of ecclesiastical unity.

SINS OF THE TONGUE

Profanity - Blasphemous or obscene language, desecrating the sacred.

Obscenity - Obscene behaviour, language or visuals.

Lies - Untruth, falsehood, fabrication, deception etc.

Detraction - The unjust damaging of another's reputation by speaking of some fault or crime of which that other is really guilty, or at any rate, is seriously believed to be guilty, by the defamer.

Calumny - The making of false and defamatory statements about someone in order to damage their reputation... *slander, defamation, character-assassination, libel etc.*

SINS OF TOUGHT

- Vanity
- Ambition
- Lustful Delectations
- Envy
- Covetousness
- Anger
- Scheming
- Treachery

SINS OF THE FLESH

Lusts of the Senses

Lustful Looks - Looking at someone with the express intention of deriving sexual pleasure from their appearance.

Double Takes - Looking at someone multiple times in order to derive sexual pleasure.

Pornography - Printed or visual material containing the explicit description or display of sexual organs or sexual activity, intended to stimulate erotic, rather than aesthetic or emotional feelings.

Lusts of the Mind

Lustful Delectations - Engaging disordered sexual thoughts for pleasure and delight.

Covetousness - Having a great desire of possessing something or someone belonging to or in an established relationship with another.

Perversions of the Flesh

Masturbation - Self-stimulation of reproductive organs for sexual pleasure.

Seduction - Tempting another towards sexual attraction.

Fornication - Sexual intercourse between unmarried individuals.

Adultery - Voluntary sexual intercourse between a married person and a person other than their spouse.

Sodomy - Sexual intercourse involving anal copulation. (*Esp. in same-sex intercourse*)

Incest - Sexual relations between people classed too closely related to marry one another.

Rape - The crime of forcing another person to have sexual intercourse against their will.

ACCESSORY TO SIN

Failure to Admonish &/or Silence - Failing to correct the sinner &/or sitting in silence while witnessing sin.

Consent &/or Approval - Agreeing to sinful schemes, language, behaviours, beliefs &/or giving expressed approval of such sin.

Encouragement &/or Excitement - Encouraging sinful behaviour or exciting it.

Provocation to Sin - Provoking someone towards sin, through dangerous language, conversation, thoughts, plans, or behaviours.

Active Participation - Actively participating in sinful conversation or behaviours etc.

Sinful Advice/Counsel - Advising someone into sinful settings, circumstances or behaviours.

Scandal - A sinful event, action, dialogue, circumstance etc. causing general public outrage.

Concealment &/or Defence of Sin - Concealing or defending obvious public sins when bound by duty to take measures against them.

Command &/or Coercion to Sin - By demanding someone, either directly or indirectly, to perform immoral acts. By threatening harm &/or the removal of some temporal good if a person does not commit a certain sin.

CONFESSIONAL GUIDE
DOGMA ON THE SACRAMENT OF PENANCE

"As a means of regaining grace and justice, penance was at all times
necessary for those who had defiled their souls with any mortal sin. . . .
Before the coming of Christ, penance was not a sacrament,
nor is it since His coming a sacrament for those who are not baptized.
But the Lord then principally instituted the Sacrament of Penance, when,
being raised from the dead, he breathed upon His disciples saying:
*'Receive ye the Holy Ghost. Whose sins you shall forgive, they are forgiven them;
and whose sins you shall retain, they are retained'* (John 20:22-23).
By which action so signal and words so clear the consent of all the Fathers
has ever understood that the power of forgiving and retaining sins
was communicated to the Apostles and to their lawful successors,
for the reconciling of the faithful who have fallen after Baptism."

COUNCIL OF TRENT
(Session XIV, c. i)

DOGMATIC CAUTIONS

"From the institution of the sacrament of penance explained,
the whole Church has always understood that the complete confession of
sins was also instituted by the Lord [*cf. Jas 5:16; 1 Jn 1:9; Lk 5:14; 17:14*]
and is divine law necessary for all who have fallen after baptism [*can. 7*].
For, when he was about to ascend from earth to heaven, our Lord Jesus
Christ left priests to represent him [*cf. Mt 16:19; 18:18; Jn 20:23*] as presiding
judges to whom all mortal sins into which the faithful of Christ would
have fallen should be brought that they, in virtue of the power of the keys,
might pronounce the sentence of remission or retention of sins.
For it is clear that without knowledge of the case, priests could not exercise
this judgement, nor could they observe equity in the imposition of
penances if the penitents declared their sins only in general
and not specifically and in particular.

Thus it follows that all mortal sins of which penitents, after a diligent self-
examination, are conscious must be recounted by them in confession...
Hence when Christ's faithful strive to confess all sins that occur to their
memory, they undoubtedly place all of them before the divine mercy for
pardon [*can. 7*]. But those who fail to do so and knowingly withhold some,
place nothing before the divine goodness for remission,
*"for if the sick is ashamed to lay open his wound before the physician,
the medicine does not heal what it does not know."*

COUNCIL OF TRENT
(Session XIV, c. v)

I. EXAMINATION OF CONSCIENCE

Prayer For Clarity:

O' Holy Spirit, come in Thy Mercy;
Enlighten my mind and strengthen my will that I may know my sins,
humbly confess them, and sincerely amend my life.

AMEN

Carefully observe the Ten Commandments of God
and the Expounded Moral Interpretation of the Catholic Church.

Write out all personal transgressions, in kind & number,
to the best of your ability.

II. ARRANGEMENTS

Schedule a confession with a Catholic Priest, or,
attend the Sacrament according to local Parish schedules.

III. SACRAMENTAL CONFESSION

In the Name of the Father, of the Son, and of the Holy Ghost.

AMEN

"Forgive me/Bless me father, for I have sinned, my last confession was…
(estimate, to the best of your ability, time elapsed since last confession)

And since that confession, I accuse myself of the following sins…

[*Recite prepared Confession… DO NOT <u>INTENTIONALLY</u> OMITT SINS…*]

For these, and all my sins which I cannot now recall, I truly am sorry and desire
God's Mercy/Pardon/Forgiveness and Reconciliation with Him."

IV. ACT OF CONTRITION

O' my God, I am truly and whole heartedly sorry for having offended Thee.
Because I dread Thy just punishments; the loss of heaven
and the pains of hell, but most of all because I have offended Thee,
my God, Whom I should love above all things.
I firmly resolve, with the help of Thy Grace, to carry out my penance,
to amend my life, to avoid the near occaisions of sin, and to sin no more.

AMEN

In the Name of the Father, of the Son, and of the Holy Ghost.
AMEN

Go Thy way in peace [Mt 9:22].

Destroy any personal notes used in Confession.

AMENDMENT OF LIFE

DETECTING PREDOMINANT FAULTS

"And lest the greatness of the revelations should exalt me, there was given [to] me a sting of my flesh, an angel of Satan, to buffet me." - **2 Cor 12:7**

Predominant Fault - The central tendency and inclination that one has towards sin as a result of worldly binds and vices. *"The spiritual or bodily thorn in one's side"* …

Most Commonly these Faults are Rooted in the Deadly Sins:

PRIDE - ANGER - LUST - ENVY - GREED - GLUTTONY - SLOTH

The Daughters of the Seven Deadly Sins (Signs / Symptoms) Aid To Detect One's Predominant Fault:

PRIDE	ANGER	LUST	ENVY
Disobedience	Indignation	Mindlessness	Hatred
Discord	Contempt	Heedlessness	Resentment
Vainglory	Hatred	Inconstancy	Gossip
Disordered	Verbal Abuse	Rashness	Detraction
Ambition	Clamor	Self-love	Sadism
Hypocrisy	Quarrelling	Hatred of God	Joy at another's misfortune
Presumption	Contumely	Worldliness	Grief at another's gain
Obstinance	Blasphemy	Despair	
Boastfulness			

GREED	GLUTTONY	SLOTH
Treachery	Unseemly Joy	Malice
Fraud	Vulgarity	Spite
Falsehood	Talkativeness	Faint-Heartedness
Perjury	Dullness of Mind	Despair
Restlessness		Sluggishness
Violence		Inattentiveness
Insensibility to Mercy		Indifferentism

SELECT REMEDIES FOR PREDOMINANT FAULTS

PRIDE	ENVY
Eucharistic Communion	Eucharistic Communion
Post-Communion Prayers & Petitions	Post-Communion Prayers & Petitions
Eucharistic Adorations	Frequent Confession
Acts of Humility - Prayers	Acts of Thanksgiving
Penitential Psalms	Acts of Poverty - Prayers
Daily Examination of Conscience	Almsgiving / Volunteering
Devotion to the Holy Face of Jesus	

LUST	ANGER
Eucharistic Communion	Eucharistic Communion
Post-Communion Prayers & Petitions	Post-Communion Prayers & Petitions
Frequent Confession	Frequent Confession
Preparation for Marriage	Eucharistic Adorations
Development within Marriage	Acts of Peace
Acts of Chastity - Prayers	Acts of Humility
Proactive Deliverance Prayers	Giving the Benefit of the Doubt
Reactive Deliverance Prayers	Charitable Estimations of Others
Devotions to the Blessed Virgin Mary	Assume the Best of Others
Novenas to the Virginal Saints	Devotions to the Sacred Heart, Holy
Invoking the Angels & Saints	Wounds, and Precious Blood of Jesus
Healing Prayers	Devotion to the Immaculate Heart of
Mortifications	Mary and the Holy Rosary
Fasting & Abstinences	Avoiding the Near Occaisions of Sin
Avoiding the Near Occaisions of Sin	Meditations on the Our Father

GREED	GLUTTONY
Eucharistic Communion	Eucharistic Communion
Post-Communion Prayers & Petitions	Post-Communion Prayers & Petitions
Frequent Confession	Frequent Confession
Acts of Thanksgiving	Bodily Mortifications
Tithing / Almsgiving / Volunteering	Fasting & Abstinences
Fasting & Abstinences	Avoiding the Near Occaisions of Sin
Reading the Books of Wisdom	Reading Sacred Scripture

SLOTH

Eucharistic Communion
Post-Communion Prayers & Petitions
Acts of Love (Prayers)
Almsgiving / Volunteering
Bodily Mortifications
Reading Sacred Scripture

AVOIDING THE NEAR OCCAISIONS OF SIN

High-Risk Occaisions of Sin - The public or private domains &/or circumstances that frequently come with strong temptations.
Ex. Internet, Television, Casinos, Bars/Pubs, Clubs, Theatres, Parties, Feasts, Entertainment, Bad company etc.

Examples of How to Avoid Occaisions of Sin:

Internet	Television
• Content Filters	• Subject Matter Reviews
• Productivity Blockers	• Content Ratings & Descriptions
• Whitelisted Sites	• Foreknowledge of Directors & Producers
• Blacklisted Sites	
• Self-Imposed Curfews	• Impose Limits to Use
• Blocked Time Intervals	• Self-Imposed Curfews
• Accountability Software	• Self-Imposed Restrictions

PROACTIVE DELIVERANCE PRAYERS
The Memorare

*Remember, O' most gracious Virgin Mary, that never was it known
that anyone who fled to thy protection, implored thy help, or sought
thy intercession, was left forsaken. Inspired with this confidence, I fly unto thee,
O' Virgin of virgins, my mother; to thee I come; before thee I stand, sinful
and sorrowful. O' Mother of the Word Incarnate, despise not
these my petitions, but in thy clemency hear and answer me.*

x3 Hail Marys
(Morning & Night)

My Mother, deliver me from all mortal sin.
AMEN

*Lord, burn our reigns and our hearts with the fire of Thy Holy Spirit,
that we may serve Thee with chaste bodies and pure minds.
Through Christ our Lord.*
AMEN

OR

*O' Lord God, King of heaven and earth, may it please Thee
this day to order and to hallow, to rule and to govern our minds,
our hearts and our bodies, thus, our thoughts, our words and our deeds,
according to Thy Law and in the doing of Thy Commandments, that we,
being helped by Thee, may here and hereafter worthily be saved & delivered
by Thee, O' Saviour of the world, Who livest and reignest for ever.*
AMEN

REACTIVE DELIVERANCE PRAYERS

For deliverance from specific evil spirits… of deadly sins etc… during Temptations.

EXAMPLES OF RELATED EVIL SPIRITS

Lust, Impurity, Adultery, Sensuality, Promiscuity, Seduction, Whoredom, Harlotry, Fornication, Voyeurism, Pornography, Effeminacy, Sexual Addiction Autoeroticism, Masturbation, Incontinence, Onanism, Seed-Wasting, Unchastity.	Anger, Rage, Violence, Bitterness, Tantrums, Quarrelling, Strife, Enmity, Division, Contention, Vengeance, Vindictiveness, Wrath, Cruelty, Misanthropy, Cynicism, Misery, Pessimism, Negativity, Sadism, Prejudice, Criticism, Resentment, Contempt, Belittling, Paranoia, Suspicion/Distrust.	Pride, Narcissism, Egoism, Self-Will, Self-Absorption, Self-Love, Arrogance, Self-Sufficiency, Self-Gratification, Vanity, Superiority, Ambition, Rebellion, Betrayal, Impulsivity, Selfishness, Hypocrisy, Religiosity, Self-Hate, Self-Loathing, Self-Destruction, Insecurity, Shyness, Timidity, Masochism.
Gluttony, Overindulgence, Drug Addiction, Alcoholism, Sexual Humour, Cussing, Crudity, Vulgarity, Detraction, Mockery, Sloth, Idleness, Hesitation, Doubt, Procrastination, Boredom, Trance, Fickleness, Inconstancy, Inconsistency, Inattention. Greed, Addiction, Gambling.	Envy, Covetousness, Jealousy, Mimicry, Detraction, Simulation, Adulation, Idolatry, Fanaticism, Manipulation, Scheming, Boasting, Bragging.	Grief, Sadness, Despair, Blues, Hopelessness, Anxiety, Stress, Fear, Withdrawal, Numbness, Seclusion/Isolation, Loneliness, Regret, Guilty, Shame, Suffocation, Scrupulosity.

In the Name of the Father, the Son, and the Holy Spirit.

By the Sign of the Cross, O' Lord, deliver us from our enemies.

AMEN

—

Spirit(s) of _________ …, I ***bind*** you in the
Most High Name of Jesus Christ, by the Power of the Holy Cross,
And by the Power of the Most Precious Blood of Our Lord Jesus Christ.
I command you to be gone from _________ …, to depart from my dwelling,
And that you flea to the foot of the Holy Cross for your just judgment! [x3]

In the Name of the Father, the Son, and the Holy Spirit.

AMEN

—

In the Most High Name of Jesus Christ , I completely & utterly ***reject***,
With the full force of my will, all spirits of _______________…
By the Power of the Holy Ghost,
And for the greater glory of God the Father. [x3]

AMEN

—

Psalms of Deliverance:

4, 5, 7, 10, 13, 17, 22, 25, 31, 34, 35, 43, 54, 59, 64, 69,
70, 91, 102, 107, 120, 140, 142, 143, 144, 146

HEALING PRAYERS & DEVOTIONS

Devotion to the Holy Face of Jesus
Rosary Chaplet of the Holy Wounds

Psalms of Healing:

6, 30, 38, 41, 42, 51, 71, 80, 85, 113, 116, 141

INVOCATIONS OF THE ANGELS & SAINTS

Prayers to St. Michael:

St. Michael the Archangel, defend us in battle.
Be our protection against the wickedness and snares of the Devil.
May God rebuke him, we humbly pray, and do thou,
O' Prince of the heavenly host, by the power of God, cast into hell
Satan and all the evil spirits, who prowl throughout the world,
seeking the ruin of souls.
AMEN

St. Michael the Archangel, defend us in battle,
lest we parish in the fear of judgement.
AMEN

Prayers to Guardian Angel:

Angel of God, my guardian dear, to whom God's love commits me here,
Ever this day (or night) be at my side, to light & guard, to rule & guide.
AMEN

Angel of God, guard my sight and mind.
Protect me from all evil spirits and lusts of the flesh.
Support my spirit, that my heart may love Christ above
the false promises of lust and those of the world.
AMEN

Novenas to the Saints:

For Chastity - Novenas to the Virginal Saints & Martyrs:
The B.V.M. + Ss. Agnes, Agatha, Anastasia, Angela, Barbara, Basil, Benedict,
Catherine, Cecilia, Clare, Maria Goretti, Veronica etc.
Novenas to the Saints who Converted from Impurity to Chastity:
Ss. Aloysius Gonzaga, Augustine, Catherine of Siena,
Mary Magdalene, Mary of Egypt, Ignatius, Justina etc.

For Temperance - *Ss. Joseph, Benedict of Nursia, Polycarp, Francis of Assisi,*
Augustine, John of the Cross, Dymphna, Sophia, Florentina etc.

For Fortitude - *Ss. Maximillian Kolbe, Anthony of Padua, Adrian of Nicodemia,*
Ignatius of Loyola, Sebastian, Daniel, George etc.

REPARATIONS FOR SIN

REPARATIONAL PRAYER & DEVOTION

Definition: The making of amends for wrongs one has done through specific prayers & devotions established by the Church for the benefit of the faithful.

Examples of Reparational Devotions

Direct	Indirect
• Indulgenced Acts • The Holy Face Devotion • Reparations to the Sacred Heart of Jesus • Holy Hour of Reparation • Reparations to the B.V.M.	• Same Devotions Offered For Sinners • Same Devotions Offered For Conversions • Same Devotions Offered For Enemies

ALMSGIVING

Definition: The practice of giving money, food, or other necessary provisions to people lacking them.

Examples of Modern Almsgiving Methods

Food & Drink	Clothes	Shelter
• Direct donations. • Prepare to give gift cards to efficient food locations. • St. Vincent De Paul Program. • Contribution to local food banks. • Volunteering at Soup Kitchens.	• Direct clothes donations. • Donations to Goodwill & / or equivalents. • Sponsorship of Children or Families.	• Hospitality to the homeless (if safe to do so). • Donation of temporary shelters. • Donation of essential supplies.

FASTING & ABSTINENCE

Definition: Abstaining from all or some kinds of food &/or drink,
esp. as a religious observance. *Denying oneself a licit good…*

Examples of Fasting & Abstinence

Abstinence	Partial Fasting	Total Fasting
• Denying oneself flesh meat as food intake. *Ex chicken, beef, pork, lamb etc.* • Denying oneself other food products like dairy, gluten, fish etc.	• Reduction of food portions for one or multiple meals in a day. • Reduction of the number of meals in a day. • Reduction of portion sizes and number of meals in a day.	• No food intake, with basic fluid intake, for a specified time period. • No food or water intake for a specified time period.

MORTIFICATIONS

Definition: The action of subduing one's bodily desires.
Natural Bodily Desires: *Libido, Thirst, Appetite, Cravings,
Desire for warmth, Desire for comfort etc.*

Examples of Mortification Against Bodily Desires

Appetite & Cravings	Desire for Warmth	Desire for Comfort
• Abstinences • Partial Fasting • Total Fasting	• Cold Showers • Ice Baths • Exposure to the Elements	• Physical Exercise • Goat Hair Celice • Hair Shirts • Firm Bed

*"And every one that striveth for the mastery, refraineth himself from
all things: and they indeed that they may receive a corruptible crown;
but we an incorruptible one. I therefore so run, not as at an uncertainty:
I so fight, not as one beating the air: But I chastise my body,
and bring it into subjection: lest perhaps, when I have preached to others,
I myself should become a castaway."*

1 Cor 9:25-27

GOOD WORKS

JESUS CHRIST

"Even so every good tree bringeth forth good fruit, and the evil tree bringeth forth evil fruit. A good tree cannot bring forth evil fruit, neither can an evil tree bring forth good fruit.
Every tree that bringeth not forth good fruit, shall be cut down, and shall be cast into the fire."

Mt 7:17-18
Lk 6:43

"And when the Son of man shall come in his majesty, and all the angels with him, then shall he sit upon the seat of his majesty. And all nations shall be gathered together before him, and he shall separate them one from another, as the shepherd separateth the sheep from the goats: And he shall set the sheep on his right hand, but the goats on his left.

Then shall the king say to them that shall be on his right hand: *'Come, ye blessed of my Father, possess you the kingdom prepared for you from the foundation of the world. For I was hungry, and you gave me to eat; I was thirsty, and you gave me to drink; I was a stranger, and you took me in: Naked, and you covered me: sick, and you visited me: I was in prison, and you came to me.'*

Then shall the just answer him, saying: *'Lord, when did we see thee hungry, and fed thee; thirsty, and gave thee drink? And when did we see thee a stranger, and took thee in? or naked, and covered thee? Or when did we see thee sick or in prison, and came to thee?'*

And the king answering, shall say to them: *'Amen I say to you, as long as you did it to one of these my least brethren, you did it to me.'*

Then he shall say to them also that shall be on his left hand: *'Depart from me, you cursed, into everlasting fire which was prepared for the devil and his angels. For I was hungry, and you gave me not to eat: I was thirsty, and you gave me not to drink. I was a stranger, and you took me not in: naked, and you covered me not: sick and in prison, and you did not visit me.'*
Then they also shall answer him, saying:
'Lord, when did we see thee hungry, or thirsty, or a stranger, or naked, or sick, or in prison, and did not minister to thee?'

Then he shall answer them, saying:
*'Amen I say to you, as long as you did it not to one of these least,
neither did you do it to me.'*
And these shall go into everlasting punishment:
but the just, into life everlasting."

Mt 25:31-46

"For the Son of man shall come in the glory of his Father
with his angels: and then will he render to every man
according to his works."

Mt 16:27

"Behold, I come quickly; and my reward is with me,
to render to every man according to his works."

Ap 22:12

CORPORAL WORKS OF MERCY	SPIRITUAL WORKS OF MERCY
• Feed the Hungry • Give Drink to the Thirsty • Clothe the Naked • Shelter the Homeless • Care for the Sick • Visit the Imprisoned • Bury the Dead	• Comfort the Sorrowful • Instruct the Ignorant • Counsel the Doubtful • Bear Wrongs Patiently • Admonish the Sinner • Forgive Injuries • Pray for the Dead
Examples: - Volunteering at Food Banks, Soup Kitchens *etc.* - Donating to Food Banks, Soup Kitchens, other programs for the poor and homeless *etc.* - Volunteering &/or Donating at Donation Centers - Direct Almsgiving - Direct Hospitality - Funding Housing Initiatives - Healthcare - Personal Support Work - Social Work - Chaplaincy - Pallbearer Work	**Examples:** - Compassion, Empathy towards Neighbour - Catechism, Religious Instruction - Bookmaking - Theological Works - Education of Family and Dependents - Preach God's Existence, Providence Mercy, Grace, Love - Fraternal Correction - Tolerance and Forbearance of Insults & Injuries - Clemency & Mercy Towards Neighbours and Enemies - Prayer for the Church Suffering

ST. JAMES
"What shall it profit, my brethren, if a man say he hath faith,
but hath not works? Shall faith be able to save him?…
So faith also, if it have not works, is dead in itself…
Do you see that by works a man is justified; and not by faith only?…
So even as the body without the spirit is dead;
so also faith without works is dead."

Jam 2:14, 17, 24, 26

ST. PAUL
"If I speak with the tongues of men, and of angels, and have not
charity, I am become as sounding brass, or a tinkling cymbal.
And if I should have prophecy and should know all mysteries,
and all knowledge, and if I should have all faith, so that I could
remove mountains, and have not charity, I am nothing.
And if I should distribute all my goods to feed the poor,
and if I should deliver my body to be burned,
and have not charity, it profiteth me nothing."

1 Cor 13:1-3

"And now there remain faith, hope, and charity,
these three: but the greatest of these is charity."

1 Cor 13:13

ST. PETER
"Therefore, my brothers and sisters, make every effort to confirm
your calling and election. For if you do these things,
you will never stumble, and you will receive a rich welcome into the
eternal kingdom of our Lord and Saviour Jesus Christ."

2 Pet 1:10

VIRTUES & VICES

THEOLOGICAL VIRTUES:
FAITH
HOPE
CHARITY / LOVE

CARDINAL VIRTUES:
PRUDENCE
TEMPERANCE
JUSTICE
FORTITUDE

SUB-VIRTUES	OPPOSING VICES
PRUDENCE: • Caution / Carefulness • Memory / Knowledge • Reason / Logic • Understanding • Acquiescence / Docility • Foresight / Provision / Attentiveness • Circumspection / Conscientiousness • Shrewdness / Tactfulness	**IMPRUDENCE:** • Recklessness / Heedlessness • Inconstancy / Double-Mindedness • Foolishness / Stupidity • Stubbornness / Pertinacity • Guile / Fraud / Deception • Negligence / Carelessness / Dereliction • Craftiness / Scheming • Worldly/Carnal Prudence
TEMPERANCE: • Meekness / Forbearance / Reticence • Clemency / Mercy / Leniency / Mildness • Humility / Modesty / Shame • Integrity / Honestia • Sobriety / Moderation • Fasting • Abstinence • Chastity / Continence • Virginity / Purity / Innocence • Simplicity / Straightforwardness / One-Mindedness • Eutrapelia (Right-Recreation) • Sportsmanship • Decorum • Silence • Studiousness / Astuteness	**INTEMPERANCE:** • Crudity • Immodesty / Shamelessness • Corruption / Deception / Depravity • Gluttony / Overindulgence • Drunkenness / Intoxication / Inebriation • Incontinence / Unchastity / Impurity • Lustfulness / Fornication • Adulterousness • Incestuousness • Anger / Cruelty • Pride / Egoism / Egocentrism • Curiosity, unmitigated

SUB-VIRTUES	OPPOSING VICES
JUSTICE: • Religion / Worship • Devotion / Constancy / Commitment • Piety / Pursuit of Sanctitude • Commutative Justice • Distributive Justice • Restitutive Justice • Legal Justice • Epikeia- Understanding Lawmakers' Intent • Patriotism / Loyalty to Country • Veneration / Giving Due-Honour • Obedience to God / Amenability / Compliance with God's Precepts • Diligence / Dutifulness • Gratitude / Thanksgiving • Just Vindication • Truthfulness / Honesty / Integrity • Affability / Friendship / Amicability • Liberality / Generosity	**INJUSTICE:** • Idolatry • Sacrilege • Superstition &/or Divination • Overvaluation of Human Respects • Violence / Murderousness • Theft / Robbery • Prejudice / Condemnations • False Accusation • Perjury • Disobedience / Misconduct / Indiscipline • Detraction &/or Contumely • Vengefulness / Spitefulness • Murmuring / Gossip • Derision / Mockery / Ridicule • Malediction / Cursing • Usury &/or Simony • Lying / Falsehood • Simulation / Hypocrrisy • Boasting / Bragging • Ingratitude / Ungratefulness / Thankless • Adulation / Flattery • Litigious / Contentious • Avaricious / Greedy / Rapacious / Covetous • Prodigality / Wasteful
FORTITUDE: • Courage / Bravery • Magnanimity / Benevolence / Charity • Magnificence / Nobility / Greatness • Patience / Resignation / Forbearance • Perseverance / Determination / Resolve • Longanimity / Endurance / Tolerance • Mortification / Toughness / Discipline	**COWARDICE:** • Fear / Anxiety • Rash Fearlessness / Recklessness • Audacity / Intrepidity • Presumption / Assumptive Expectation • Ambition • Inane Glory / Vainglory • Pusillanimity / Timidity • Stinginess / Cheapness / Miserliness • Effeminacy / Softness • Pertinacity / Tenacious / Dogged

STAGES OF SANCTIFICATION

THE PURGATIVE STATE
"The first stage of Sainthood"

- The sinner recognizes the veracity of the Eternal Law, making clear admission of personal transgressions and is struck with terror at the prospect of damnation.
- The sinner actively seeks justification by Christ alone, and the channels established by Christ for Grace & Mercy (viz. baptism &/or confession etc).
- Despite receiving the Sanctifying Grace of God, the remission of personal sins, and the gift of the Holy Spirit, the sinner retains certain attachments to pre-conversion sins and falls into them, or other serious sins. This may occur *frequently* in the beginning, and only *occasionally* with great progress.
- The sinner is perseverant in repenting when fallen, revisiting the Tribunal of Mercy as needed, without unnecessary delay.
- The sinner advances past this stage of sanctification when ceasing to commit mortal sins *occasionally*, but only *rarely*, while still committing venial sins, even *frequently*.

THE ILLUMINATIVE STATE

- The sinner no longer retains the same pre-conversion attachments to mortal sins and has developed a disgust for them, similar in likeness to the abhorrence that God has for sin, although in lesser degree.
- As a result, the sinner does not return to the filth of mortal sin, so long as it is regarded as such. It remains possible still, to lapse into past ways.
- The sinner still retains certain predispositions to venial sins and may commit them *frequently*.
- Advancing in this stage of sanctification, the sinner aims further by co-operating with the Grace of God in order to root out & quell personal imperfections, iniquities and disordered passions.
- Venial sins begin to drop off markedly in the latter stages of this state.

THE UNITIVE STATE

- Very rare to attain to in this life on earth, the unitive state is akin to the state that Adam & Eve lived in with God before their Fall.
- The soul walks in friendship with God, having inadvertent faults, however, purification of Soul in regard to iniquities and disordered passions has been achieved.

REFERENCES

Catholic Church. (1994). *Catechism of the Catholic Church.* 1st Image Books ed. Crown Publishing Group.

Catholic Church. Hünermann, P., Hoping, H., Fastiggi, R. L., Nash, A. E., & Denzinger, H. (2012). *Compendium of creeds, definitions, and declarations on matters of faith and morals* (43rd ed.). Ignatius Press.

Catholic Church. Poenitentiaria Apostolica. The Raccolta; or, A Manual of Indulgences, Prayers, and Devotions Enriched with Indulgences in Favor of All the Faithful in Christ or of Certain Groups of Persons, and Now Opportunely Revised, Edited and in Part Newly Translated into English from the 1950 Official "Enchiridion Indulgentiarum--Preces Et Pia Opera" Issued by the Sacred Penitentiary Apostolic. New York: Benziger Bros., 1952.

Challoner, R. (2000). *The Holy Bible: Translated from the Latin Vulgate: Diligently compared with the Hebrew, Greek and other editions in divers languages: The Old Testament, first published by the English College at Douay, A.D. 1609, and the New Testament, first published by the English College at Rheims, A.D. 1582: With annotations, references, and an historical and chronological index.* Tan Books and Publishers.

Denzinger, H., Hoping, H., Hünermann, P., Fastiggi, R. L., & Nash, A. E. (2012). *Compendium of creeds, definitions, and declarations on matters of faith and morals.* Ignatius Press.

Fr. Chad Ripperger, *Sermon on the Levels of Prayer.* (2018). Sensus Fidelium.

Fr. Chad Ripperger, *Moral Virtues (and Opposing Vices).* (2016). Sensus Traditionis.

Jurgens, S.P. (2004). *The Roman Catholic Daily Missal, 1962.* Angelus Press.

The New Oxford American Dictionary. (2005). Oxford University Press.

Made in the USA
Monee, IL
02 April 2025

15091014R00056